总顾问：牛　健　丁国声
总主编：任静生

职场综合英语教程（第二册）

主　编：张　荣
副主编：史雯娜　孙　维　施佳佳
编　者：陈　婧　王　璠　易雅琼　徐　萍
　　　　黄海燕　袁　平　吴　翔　章素华

北京大学出版社
PEKING UNIVERSITY PRESS

图书在版编目(CIP)数据

职场综合英语教程(第二册)/张荣主编.—北京：北京大学出版社，2013.1
（全国职业技能英语系列教材）
ISBN 978-7-301-20798-7

Ⅰ.①职… Ⅱ.①张… Ⅲ.①英语–高等职业教育–教材 Ⅳ.①H31

中国版本图书馆CIP数据核字(2012)第127631号

书　　　名：职场综合英语教程（第二册）
著作责任者：张　荣　主编
策　　　划：谢尚楒　万晶晶
责 任 编 辑：郝妮娜
标 准 书 号：ISBN 978-7-301-20798-7/H·3074
出 版 发 行：北京大学出版社
地　　　址：北京市海淀区成府路205号　100871
网　　　址：http://www.pup.cn　新浪官方微博：@北京大学出版社
电 子 信 箱：zbing@pup.pku.edu.cn
电　　　话：邮购部 62752015　发行部 62750672　编辑部 62759634　出版部 62754962
印　　　刷　者：北京大学印刷厂
经　　　销　者：新华书店
　　　　　　　　787毫米×1092毫米　16开本　11.25印张　330千字
　　　　　　　　2013年1月第1版　2015年11月第5次印刷
定　　　价：45.00元（附光盘）

未经许可，不得以任何方式复制或抄袭本书之部分或全部内容。
版权所有，侵权必究　举报电话：010-62752024
　　　　　　　　　电子信箱：fd@pup.pku.edu.cn

前　言

职业化已经成为高职高专教育最显著的特征。增加实训、强调动手能力、采用"订单式"培养模式是其主要特色。在这种背景下,按照传统的教学方法进行基础课教学已经不容置疑的受到了挑战。就目前情况论,高职高专的基础课教学必须践行"以服务为宗旨,以就业为导向"的专业建设指导思想。在课程建设以及基础课教学内容中,必须结合学生的专业需求,有意识地融入与职场相关联的知识。

根据教育部《高职高专英语教育课程教学基本要求》的精神,联合国家级示范高职院校和骨干高职院校的一线教师,在充分调查现有高职高专英语教材的基础上,结合高职英语教学的未来发展趋势,在"安徽省高职高专外语教研会"的组织及北京大学出版社的支持下,编写了本套《职场综合英语教程》,并被列入普通高等教育"十二五"规划教材。

本套教程分为基础篇、第一册、第二册和第三册,共四册。

基础篇　主要针对英语基础比较薄弱的学生,融入了对音标的训练,旨在帮助这部分学生巩固英语的基础知识,为后续课程的学习奠定必要的基础。

第一册　主要涉及西方文化和日常生活,内容涵盖西方名人、青年旅馆、主题公园、肥皂剧、网上购物等。鲜活的内容、生活化的主题,有利于学生顺利融入大学生活,同时也有助于培养学生对英语学习的兴趣,为今后的职业化过渡打下坚实基础。

第二册　主要涉及求职以及职业素养培养等主题,如求职、自主创业、职场中人际交往和做好服务、科技与生活、名人的成功与失败等。另外,本册内容与职场文化的有机融合有利于学生对未来职业规划形成初步的认识。

第三册　从职场生活出发,针对高职学生可能遇到的职场活动进行设计,内容包括机场接待、银行服务、汽车制造等。内容难度适中,选材谨慎,真正做到通识化与职场化有机统筹,有助于学生以后进一步学习相关的专业英语。

本套教材的内容主要分为六个方面:听说、阅读、语法、应用文写作、文化速递与拓展词汇。

听说部分　践行任务型教学的指导思想,强调能听懂简单对话,能记录关键词,能就所给事物说出英语名称,或进行角色分工,完成简单对话。这部分设计了热身环节,通过比较容易完成的任务,帮助学生尽快进入相关主题的学习。而角色扮演部分则试图充分调动学生的想象力和创造力,按照角色分工完成任务。听说部分还设计了听写内容,旨在培养学生听懂并记录关键词的能力。

阅读部分　　由两篇相关主题的文章组成,其中第一篇为主要文章,教师应该进行精深讲解;第二篇属于附加文章,教师可以把它作为泛读教材使用。目的是让学生在阅读过程中完成对该主题的英语核心词汇的巩固和学习,同时深刻理解英语的语句结构。

语法部分　　旨在夯实高职高专学生的语法基础,改善语法能力薄弱的现状,同时结合"高等学校英语应用能力考试"要求,对一些考试技巧进行精解,真正做到融会贯通,为提高英语综合能力打下良好基础。

写作部分　　紧扣职场,重在应用文的写作。提供较规范的写作模式与常用句型供学生参考,通过实际的操练让学生进一步熟悉并掌握多种应用文的写作。

文化速递　　是本套教材的特色之一。是针对单元主题的拓展性学习资料,可以帮助学生开阔视野、拓展知识面,提高综合人文素养。

词汇部分　　依据大纲要求,课文中涉及的生词均分级标出。标★为A级词汇,标☆为超纲词汇。方便教师把握教学重点,也方便学生分级掌握词汇,逐步进级。

配有教学课件　　每个单元针对不同的主题都有话题的进一步延伸,有利于教师进行拓展教学。丰富授课内容,活跃课堂气氛,激发学生的学习兴趣。

本套教材得到教育部高等学校高职高专英语类专业教学指导委员会的悉心指导,由教指委秘书长牛健博士和副主任委员丁国声教授担任总顾问,由安徽新华学院外国语学院院长任静生教授担任总主编,国家示范性高等职业院校芜湖职业技术学院、安徽水利水电职业技术学院、安徽职业技术学院、安庆职业技术学院等院校的英语教学专家负责编写任务;明尼苏达大学商业管理Brian Meyer博士以及天津外国语大学等院校的专家为此套教材的出版倾注了大量的心血;其他参编人员及编辑老师们也付出了巨大的努力,在此谨向他们表示衷心的感谢。

高职高专英语教学任重道远,教材建设未有止境。本套教材的出版旨在探索新形势下高职高专英语教学的一条教学新路。缺点与不足之处在所难免,衷心希望得到专家学者的批评指正,听到广大师生的改进意见。

编者
2012年12月

Contents

Unit 1　Job Hunting ·· 1
    Part Ⅰ　Listening and Speaking / 2
    Part Ⅱ　Reading / 5
        Text A　5 Sure-fire Ways to Mess up a Job Interview / 6
        Text B　Challenging Job Market in China / 10
    Part Ⅲ　Strategies: 听力解析 / 15
    Part Ⅳ　Applied Writing: Resume(简历) / 17
    Part Ⅴ　Cultural Express: Job Hunting Tips / 19

Unit 2　Interesting Jobs ·· 22
    Part Ⅰ　Listening and Speaking / 23
    Part Ⅱ　Reading / 27
        Text A　Event Planning: Wedding / 27
        Text B　Premarital Counseling / 32
    Part Ⅲ　Strategies: 词汇解析 / 35
    Part Ⅳ　Applied Writing: Contract (合同) / 40
    Part Ⅴ　Cultural Express: Trying Different Jobs vs. Taking a Long Term Career / 43

Unit 3　Business on Campus ·· 46
    Part Ⅰ　Listening and Speaking / 47
    Part Ⅱ　Reading / 50
        Text A　To Be the Next Millionaire / 51
        Text B　Money Making Schemes / 55
    Part Ⅲ　Strategies: 翻译解析 / 58
    Part Ⅳ　Applied Writing: Specifications (说明书) / 60
    Part Ⅴ　Cultural Express: Tips on Starting an E-Business / 61

Unit 4　Customer Service 64

Part Ⅰ　Listening and Speaking / 65
Part Ⅱ　Reading / 69
　　　Text A　The Greatest Customer Service Story Ever Told / 69
　　　Text B　Rules for Good Customer Service / 74
Part Ⅲ　Strategies: 写作解析 / 77
Part Ⅳ　Applied Writing: Complaint Letter (投诉信) / 80
Part Ⅴ　Cultural Express: Wal-Mart Business Culture / 81

Unit 5　Culture Shock 84

Part Ⅰ　Listening and Speaking / 85
Part Ⅱ　Reading / 90
　　　Text A　Disney Culture Shock / 91
　　　Text B　How to Handle Business Culture Shock / 96
Part Ⅲ　Strategies: 阅读解析（一）/ 100
Part Ⅳ　Applied Writing: Welcome Speech/Letter (欢迎词) / 107
Part Ⅴ　Cultural Express: Cross-Cultural Differences / 109
　　　　　　　　　　　　Travel in China / 110

Unit 6　Technology and Life 113

Part Ⅰ　Listening and Speaking / 114
Part Ⅱ　Reading / 118
　　　Text A　How Has Technology Changed Our Lives / 118
　　　Text B　How did the iPad Change Our Lives? / 122
Part Ⅲ　Strategies: 阅读解析（二）/ 125
Part Ⅳ　Applied Writing: Farewell Speech/Letter (欢送词) / 128
Part Ⅴ　Cultural Express：What is Intercultural Communication？/ 130
　　　　　　　　　　　　German or Global? / 130

Unit 7　Elite Entrepreneurs 132

Part Ⅰ　Listening and Speaking / 133
Part Ⅱ　Reading / 138
　　　Text A　Henry Ford—Founder of the Ford Motor Company / 139
　　　Text B　Huayi Brothers and the New Business of Chinese
　　　　　　　Blockbusters / 144
Part Ⅲ　Strategies: 阅读解析（三）/ 148

    Part Ⅳ   Applied Writing: Advertisement (广告) / 149
    Part Ⅴ   Cultural Express：Microsoft Corporation / 152

Unit 8 Failure and Success 154
    Part Ⅰ   Listening and Speaking / 155
    Part Ⅱ   Reading / 159
             Text A   *Looking Back and Looking Forward* / 159
             Text B   *Love and Loss* / 163
    Part Ⅲ   Strategies: 阅读解析（四）/ 167
    Part Ⅳ   Applied Writing: Memo (备忘录) / 169
    Part Ⅴ   Cultural Express：Apple / 170

Unit 1

Job Hunting

Learning Objectives:

You are able to:
☞ Design a resume
☞ Write an application letter

You are suggested to:
☞ Recognize the English terms for different positions
☞ Be familiar with some well-known companies

Part I Listening and Speaking

Warm-up

Task 1

Directions: Do you know their Chinese meanings? Try to say something about them.

| blouse | dress | high-heeled shoes | handbag | tie |
| briefcase | watch | necklace | lighter | tie-clip |

(1) (2) (3) (4) (5) (6) (7) (8) (9) (10)

Task 2

Directions: Work with your partner and match the following Chinese phrases with their English equivalents.

推荐信 ☆
成绩单 ☆
毕业证书 ☆
初级工作 ☆
团队工作能力 ☆
推荐人 ☆
学位证书 ☆
简历 ☆

★ school transcripts
★ team player (worker)
★ entry-level work
★ a letter of recommendation
★ graduate certificate
★ resume
★ diploma
★ referee

Oral Practice

Task 1

Directions: Read the dialogue and answer the questions.

Ivy: Which school are you attending?
Alice: I am attending Hebei University of Technology.
Ivy: When will you graduate from that university?
Alice: This coming July.
Ivy: What degree will you receive?

Unit 1 Job Hunting

Alice: I will receive a Bachelor's degree.
Ivy: What is your major?
Alice: My major is Business Administration.
Ivy: How have you been getting on with your studies so far?
Alice: I have been doing quite well at college. According to the academic records I've achieved so far, I am confident that I will receive my Bachelor of Business Administration degree this coming July.

1. When will Alice graduate from that university?
   ☐ This July   ☐ Next July
2. What is Alice's major?
   ☐ Business Management   ☐ Business Administration
3. Why is Alice so confident with herself?
   ☐ She has achieved a good academic standing at college.
   ☐ She will receive the Bachelor of Business Administration degree.

Task 2

Directions: Suppose you are the interviewee for the position of computer technician in a company, your partner is an interviewer. Use the information in the following Resume and role-play an interview with your partner. Then reverse the role and do it again.

Listening Practice

Task 1

Directions: Listen to an interview and tick (√) in the box at the end of the correct answer.

1. The age of the interviewee is_____.
   A. 24 years old ☐
   B. 25 years old ☐
   C. 26 years old ☐
2. The interviewee was born in_____.
   A. Beijing ☐
   B. Nanjing ☐
   C. Tianjin ☐
3. The interviewee is now living in_____.
   A. 606 Zhongguancun Road, Apt 802, Beijing ☐
   B. 660 Zhongguancun Road, Apt 820, Beijing ☐
   C. 666 Zhongguancun Road, Apt 802, Beijing ☐
4. The interviewee is_____.
   A. single ☐
   B. married ☐
   C. divorced ☐
5. In the interviewee's family there are_____.
   A. her parents, her elder sister and her ☐
   B. her parents, her younger sister and her ☐
   C. her parents, her elder brother and her ☐

Task 2

Directions: In this section you will hear a recorded short passage. The passage will be read three times. You are required to put the missing words or phrases in the numbered blanks according to what you hear.

There are (1)_____ other types of vocational schools in Germany. The first one is the (2)_____ School, a full-time secondary vocational school. These schools do not (3)_____ any tuition fees. The course at this type of school lasts 1—3 years. This type of education prepares the students for special (4)_____ trainings. Students can also get a (5)_____ graduation at the school. The second additional (6)_____ of German vocational schools is the (7)_____ School, a full-time or part-time post-secondary vocational school, and also most often a (8)_____ school. Only graduates of a vocational school, with (often) at least 1 year (9)_____ experience after graduation, are permitted to attend this type of school. The (10)_____ at a Training school lasts 1—2 years for full-time students and 2—4 years for part-time students.

Task 3

Directions: Listen to a conversation and work with your partner to fill in the blanks of the form given below.

Candidate Form

1. Name of Candidate : _____
2. Age : _____
3. Sex : _____
4. The position of the job you want to apply for : _____
5. How did you get the information about this job : _____

Part II Reading

Text A

Before Reading:

Seeing the following pictures, can you tell what they do for a living?

5 Sure-fire Ways to Mess up a Job Interview

Whether it's your first interview or just another one of many, there's always a chance that you'll mess up. Even the most skilled interviewees have experienced a bad interview where they've left with their tail between their legs. Employers are aware of the fact that interviewees experience huge pressure and understand that stress can cause them to make mistakes. There are, however, some things which can instantly put off an employer and ruin your chances of getting hired, regardless of what your CV has to offer.

Everyone has certain habits, which is quite normal, but you should try to stop them during a job interview. Biting your nails due to nervousness won't do too much harm, but picking your nose or other body parts really isn't recommended. You may not notice you have these bad habits, so try a practice interview with a friend or family member who can identify any bad habits for you to eliminate.

Avoid bad mouthing and complaining about previous employers, even if it was the reason you left your job. Pushing the blame doesn't make you look good, rather it creates the image that you're a troublesome employee. Think of another reason to provide your interviewer with when questioned about previous jobs. Simply saying the job wasn't for you might be enough.

Getting your interviewer's name and title wrong can cause offense and certainly won't win you any bonus points. If you're unsure about their names and titles, it's best to leave them out. Avoid piling additional pressure onto yourself, just concentrate on remaining calm and in control.

Nothing gives off a worst impression than showing up to a job interview late—it shows lack of responsibility and little motivation. Aim to arrive at least fifteen minutes early and give yourself extra time if you're unsure of the exact location.

In some cases, unexpected situations can cause you to be late for an interview or unable to attend and employers do understand this can happen. What really bothers them is if you haven't informed them of your situation so they can either reschedule you in for another time or continue with other work while they wait for you. If there's been an accident on the motorway or a family member falls sick, call and apologize, explain the situation and reschedule the interview. Always make sure you tell them you're still interested in the position and that you regret the situation has arisen at an unfortunate time.

Confidence is a positive quality which can help you do well in the job interview but arrogance is not. Arrogance can really discourage a potential employer from hiring you as you'll appear difficult to manage and unlikely to follow instruction. Make sure you're eager and attentive during your interview and demonstrate that you're listening by making eye contact with them.

Avoid using coarse language or expressing contradicting views—both inside and outside of the interview room. There's plenty of time for those things once you've been hired...

(495 words)

Unit 1 Job Hunting

New Words

(标★为A级词汇,标☆为超纲词汇)

☆interviewee	/ˈɪntəvjuːiː/	n.	被接见者;被访问者
pressure	/ˈprɛʃə/	n.	压(力);压力;气压(或血压)(的缩略形式);压迫(感)
stress	/strɛs/	n.	强调;重音;压力;重力
offer	/ˈɒfə/	vt.	提供,给予;提出,提议;出价,开价;表示愿意
recommend	/rekəˈmɛnd/	vt.	推荐;劝告;使显得吸引人;托付
★eliminate	/ɪˈlɪmɪneɪt/	vt.	消除;根除(尤指不需要之物)
previous	/ˈpriːvɪəs/	adj.	先前的;以前的;过早的;(时间上)稍前的
employee	/emplɔɪˈiː, emˈplɔɪiː, ɪm-/	n.	雇工,雇员,职工
offense	/əˈfens/	n.	犯罪,违反;冒犯,触怒;攻击
bonus	/ˈbəʊnəs/	n.	奖金,额外津贴;红利,额外股息;退职金;额外令人高兴的事情
pile	/paɪl/	n.	桩;一堆;绒头;垛
		vt.	堆起;堆叠;放置;装入
		vi.	蜂拥,拥挤
situation	/sɪtjʊˈeɪʃ(ə)n/	n.	(人的)情况;局面,形势,处境;位置;[心理学]情境
reschedule	/riːˈʃɛdjuːl, -ˈskɛd-/	vt.	重新安排;重新计划
inform	/ɪnˈfɔːm/	vt.	通知
arise	/əˈraɪz/	vi.& vt.	产生;出现;起身,起立;起源于,产生于
★discourage	/dɪsˈkʌrɪdʒ/	vt.	使气馁;使沮丧;阻碍;劝阻
★potential	/pə(ʊ)ˈtɛnʃ(ə)l/	adj.	潜在的,有可能的
★contradict	/kɒntrəˈdɪkt/	vt.	反驳,驳斥;否认;与……矛盾,与……抵触
★demonstrate	/ˈdɛmənstreɪt/	vt.	证明,证实;论证;显示,展示;演示,说明

Phrases and Expressions

mess up	弄乱,弄糟
be aware of	知道,意识到
concentrate on	专心于,把思想集中于;将……集中于……

Proper Names

Sure-fire: 确切的
5 Sure-fire Ways to Mess up A Job Interview: 五种做法肯定砸了你的面试
leave with their tail between their legs: 夹着尾巴离开
CV: curriculum vitae (拉丁语) 简历

Exercises

I. Reading Comprehension

Directions: Circle the right answer for the following questions.

1. Why do interviewees often make mistakes in the interviews?
    A. Because it is their first interview.
    B. Because the employers give them a lot of pressure.
    C. Because they have huge pressure from the job interview and become very nervous.
    D. Because they don't prepare the CV well.
2. Which one is not the behavior the interviewees should avoid in an interview?
    A. Biting the nails.
    B. Being aware of bad habits.
    C. Picking the nose.
    D. Pushing the blame.
3. If the interviewees are unsure about the interviewer's names and titles, _____.
    A. they can ask them before the interview
    B. they should keep calm and be in control
    C. they should concentrate on them
    D. they can give themselves a lot of pressure
4. Which should the interviewees not do if they have an unexpected reason for being late?
    A. Inform the interviewers of the situation.
    B. Tell the interviewers you're still interested in the position.
    C. Call the interviewers and ask them to wait for you.
    D. Regret the situation has arisen at an unfortunate time.
5. The interviewees should not be _____ in the interview.
    A. eager
    B. arrogant
    C. attentive
    D. confident

II. Word Usage

Directions: Complete each of the following sentences with the correct form of the italicized word given in the brackets.

1. A phone _____ *(interview)* saves time.
2. I have _____ *(inform)* them of an urgent meeting.
3. I must _____ *(concentrate)* on my work now.
4. _____ *(pressure)* of time meant that he became adept at writing in railway carriages.
5. Who _____ *(be in control)* of the project?
6. The dispute has scared away _____ *(potential)* investors.
7. The _____ *(situation)* suddenly became tense.
8. The library is now _____ *(offer)* computer service.
9. What about the _____ *(bonus)* in your company?
10. John was _____ *(eager)* to invite us to the party.

III. Blank Filling

Directions: Translate the Chinese part of the following sentences with the correct form of the words or expressions in the box.

| mess up | be aware of | concentrate on | interviewee | eliminate |
| previous | offense | pile | reschedule | demonstrate |

1. After the fun he's had during the holidays, the boy can't _____ his school work. (集中注意力)
2. Can we ever _____ poverty from the world? (消除)
3. If I _____, I would probably be fired. (搞砸了)
4. The teacher examined the students on the _____ lesson. (前面学过的课)
5. As time went on, people came to _____ the seriousness of China's population size. (认识到)
6. What questions, usually, will an interviewer ask an _____? (应试者)
7. _____ the leaves in the corner of the yard. (堆)
8. Let me _____ to you how this machine works. (演示)
9. Because it was his first _____, the punishment wasn't too severe. (初犯)
10. I'd appreciate it if we could _____ our Wednesday meeting. (重新安排)

IV. Translation

Directions: Put the following English sentences into Chinese.

1. Your advice will make my job-hunting a lot easier in the future.
2. The interviewer will judge the interviewee's attitude by asking the motivation of the interviewee.
3. He was very nervous during his first job interview, which was understandable.
4. My resume shows that I have the right qualifications for the job.
5. I learned of the position through a newspaper advertisement.

V. True or False

Directions: Decide whether the following statements are true or false according to the text. Write "T" if the statement is true and "F" if it is false.

_____ 1. The interviewees should practice the interview, so they can be relaxed before the real one.

_____ 2. The previous employers are the reason for the interviewees leaving their former jobs.

_____ 3. Getting the interviewer's name and title will not do any help in the interview.

_____ 4. Being late to an interview shows lack of responsibility and little motivation.

_____ 5. Once the interviewees get out of the interview room, they can express contradicting views.

Text B

Before Reading:

1. What are you going to do after graduation?
2. What kind of job do you expect to get and why?

Challenging Job Market in China

When Chelsea Cai graduated from university this year (2008), she had no idea the job market would be quite so depressing. Over the past three months, Cai, a graduate of Shanghai Jiao Tong University, has sent out over 50 résumés to different companies and has managed to land interviews with seven. She has attended on-campus recruitment fairs and competed with thousands of students for positions with companies who are only looking to fill a few spots. So far, Cai, a food science and engineering major, has received one offer as a research assistant from a company that specializes in producing MSG, but has dismissed the monthly salary of RMB 2,500 as too low.

Cai is waiting to hear the results from another recent interview with a state-owned organic food producer, but she, like many of her peers, is getting increasingly frustrated.

"I've had enough of job hunting. I'm sending out résumés every day and am getting no replies, and it is just one disappointment after another. I was not prepared for this when I got out of school," says Cai.

Despite top grades and test scores, Cai continues to worry about her credentials. "At first, before I started looking for jobs, I was confident and thought I would do well, but now I don't think I'm as qualified as I thought. There is just too much competition," she says.

Cai is one of 6.1 million students who will graduate from Chinese universities this year, an increase from the 5.6 million students who graduated in 2008 and nearly six times as many as in 2000. State sources predict that, by 2011, the number of Chinese university graduates will reach 7.6 million. University graduates have been facing difficulties in finding jobs for years. The problem doesn't stem only from economic slowdown or too many people holding university degrees, but is due to a variety of different factors,

First, not only are there fewer jobs available because of the economic slowdown, but widespread cutbacks means there are more experienced people in the market who are competing for the same jobs as fresh graduates than in previous years.

Second, industries that have a high demand for workers have a comparatively low educational and skills requirement, and pay much lower wages. China's 9 to 10 percent economic growth in recent years has relied on industries that use laborers with low technical skills rather than university graduates. The nation's industrial structure cannot absorb so many university graduates; it has a greater demand for migrant workers instead.

Third, there are considerable differences in the development levels between the country's coastal region and interior, western areas. Most graduates seek jobs in the big cities in China's eastern regions, where the employment market is already relatively saturated.

Generating enough jobs for the masses of eager young students emerging from the country's universities has been a chief concern of the country's top decision makers for years. Since 1999, the number of college graduate students in China has grown by approximately 30 percent a year; as a result, the job market has been unable to keep pace with the surge of graduates entering each year.

(525 words)

New Words

（标★为A级词汇，标☆为超纲词汇）

★depressing	/dɪˈprɛsɪŋ/	adj.	令人忧愁的，使人沮丧的；使情绪低落的 (depress v.)
offer	/ˈɒfə/	n.	提议；出价，开价
★assistant	/əˈsɪst(ə)nt/	n.	助手，助理；
dismiss	/dɪsˈmɪs/	vt.	解雇，把……免职；遣散，解散（队伍等）；驳回，拒绝受理；搁置
organic	/ɔːˈɡanɪk/	adj.	有机(体)的；有组织的，系统的；器官的；根本的
☆credential	/krɪˈdɛnʃ(ə)l/	n.	外交使节所递的国书，信任状
qualified	/ˈkwɒlɪfʌɪd/	adj.	有资格的，胜任的，适当的，合格的；过检定的，得到许可的；有限制的，有条件的；
stem	/stɛm/	vt.	遏制[阻止]（液体的流动等）；阻止；封堵；遏止
cutback	/ˈkʌtbak/	n.	削减，缩减
structure	/ˈstrʌktʃə/	n.	结构；构造；建筑物；体系
★absorb	/əbˈzɔːb, -ˈsɔːb/	vt.	吸收（液体、气体等）；吸引（注意）；吞并，合并；忍受，承担（费用）
migrant	/ˈmʌɪɡr(ə)nt/	n.	候鸟；移居者，移民；随季节迁移的工作者；迁移动物
		adj.	移居的；流浪的；
★interior	/ɪnˈtɪərɪə/	adj.	内部的，内的，室内的；内地的，国内的；内面的，内心的，秘密的；本质的
☆saturate	/ˈsatʃəreɪt/	vt.	浸湿，浸透；使充满；[化]使饱和；使渗进，使湿透
generate	/ˈdʒɛnəreɪt/	vt.	形成，造成；产生物理反应；产生（后代）；引起
approximately	/əˈprɒksɪmətli/	adv.	近似地，大约
surge	/səːdʒ/	n.	汹涌；大浪，波涛

Phrases and Expressions

food science and engineering major	食品工程专业
MSG: Monosodium glutamate	味精

Unit 1 Job Hunting

Exercises

I. Summary

Directions: Fill in the blanks with the appropriate words according to your understanding.

The job market in China has been (1) _____ to keep pace with the surge of graduates (2) _____ each year. University graduates have been facing (3) _____ in job hunting for years. A lot of factors (4) _____ this problem: First, many (5) _____ people in the job market are competing for the same jobs with the (6) _____. Second, industries have a great demand for workers who have a lower educational and technical (7) _____, and pay much lower wages than graduates. Third, different regions and (8) _____ have different job markets. Most graduates have met more competitions in some big cities in China's (9) _____ regions. This is a serious problem for the country's top (10) _____ to solve.

II. Reading Comprehension

Directions: Circle the right answer for the following questions according to the text.

1. Which one is not true about Chelsea Cai?
   A. She was graduated from Shanghai Jiao Tong university.
   B. She was still confident about job hunting after graduation.
   C. She was waiting for the results from a state-owned organic food producer.
   D. She had attended recruitment fairs when she was in the university.
2. Which one is not the reason that university graduates face many difficulties in hunting jobs?
   A. economic slowdown
   B. many competitors
   C. fewer jobs available
   D. high job requirements
3. Why do industries use laborers rather than university graduates?
   A. They have enough technical skills
   B. They are paid much lower wages
   C. They have enough technical background
   D. They are more experienced.
4. Which is not the popular place for most graduates seeking jobs?
   A. eastern regions   B. coastal region   C. western areas   D. developed areas
5. Which one is true according to the passage?
   A. Recently the country's top decision makers are aware of the problem.
   B. The serious situation of job hunting frustrates the university graduates.
   C. The university graduates are more competitive than the workers in the job market.
   D. The job market is keeping pace with the wave of graduates entering the workforce.

III. Vocabulary & Structures

Directions: Fill in the blanks with the proper expressions in the box.

assistant	dismiss	qualified	stem	cutback
absorb	migrant	approximately	interior	generate

1. The way animals _____ nutrition(营养) from food can be quite different from human beings'.
2. You must _____ the flow of blood from the wound.
3. In consequence of your bad work I am forced to _____ you.
4. The people attending the convention also _____ more business in the hotel's restaurants, bars and shops.
5. He recognized that he was not _____ to be a teacher.
6. People are concerned about the _____ in welfare programs.
7. _____ workers move from country to country in search of work.
8. An _____ one day a week would ease my workload.
9. The architect laid out the _____ of the building.
10. Our English teacher is _____ in her forties.

IV. Translation

Directions: Put the following English sentences into Chinese.

1. They also let students know about job openings and job recruitment fairs.
2. My major subject is accounting and my minor subject is foreign trade.
3. Competition has forced out many small firms.
4. The job, for a university graduate, is one of the most concerning issues today.
5. Gain a distinct professional advantage in a competitive job market.

Part III Strategies

Unit 1 Job Hunting

听力解析

听力理解分为问题、对话和短文听写三个部分。问题、对话部分共10个单项选择,每道题后附4个备选答案,短文听写部分共5题填空。

1. 地点题

【试题特点】地点题提问的是对话发生的地点,常用的提问方式有:

Where does the conversation most probably take place?

Where does this conversation most likely occur?

Where are the two speakers?

【答题技巧】地点题的解答需要抓住与特定地点相关的常用词语。这类题目的对话中一般不会提到具体场所,问题往往要求根据对话内容推测出谈话场所或某人的去向。考生要注意抓取信息词,即与特定地点相关的最常用词语。

其次,考生需要熟悉常考的地点和不同场景下人们的谈话用语,这对做好地点题很有帮助。

【典型例题】

【例1】　　A) At a clinic.　　B) In a supermarket.
　　　　　C) At a restaurant.　　D) In an ice cream shop.

W: I'll have the steak, French fries, and let's see, chocolate ice cream for dessert.

M: Oh, oh, you know these things will ruin your health, too much fat and sugar, how about ordering some vegetables and fruit instead?

Q: Where does the conversation most probably take place?

【解析】从四个选项中可以看出,本题是一道地点题。在对话中出现了该题的关键词dessert和ordering,因此可以判断这一对话应当发生在餐馆里面。

2. 人物关系或身份职业题

【试题特点】

(1) 对人物关系的提问

人物关系题常用的提问方式有:

What's the probable relationship between the two speakers?

(2) 对人物职业的提问

身份职业题常用的提问方式有:

Who is the man/the woman?

【答题技巧】

在解答人物关系和身份职业题时,一定要注意双方的称呼语。对话中的称呼语往往会直接暴露出说话人的身份或说话双方的关系,比如Mr.一词就表明对方很可能是自己的上级或老师。

同时要善于捕捉关键词及人物语气。解答这类试题,不但要熟悉体现某种人物关系或某种职业的相关词汇,而且要注意说话人的语气和态度,比如师生之间、夫妻之间、家长与孩子之间以及老板与员工之间的说话方式和语气均有自己的特点。

在短对话部分常考的职业身份有:

教授(professor)、秘书(secretary)、医生(doctor)、老板(boss)、服务员(waiter/waitress)、主人(host/hostess)、修理工(repairer)、管道工/水暖工(plumber)、电工(electrician)、家庭角色(husband/wife/son/daughter/girlfriend...)

短对话部分涉及的人物关系包括:

夫妻(husband—wife)、父子(father—son)、母子(mother—son)、师生(teacher—student)、同学(schoolmate/classmate)、同事(colleague)、老板与秘书(boss—secretary)、雇主与雇员(employer—employee)、医生与病人(doctor—patient)、服务员与顾客(waiter/waitress—customer)、主人与客人(host/hostess—guest)、警察与司机(policeman—driver)、管理员与借阅者(librarian—reader)、房东与租房者(landlord/landlady—tenant)

【典型例题】

【例2】A) A bank clerk.   B) A secretary.   C) A landlady.   D) A doctor.

M: According to your ad. in this morning's paper, you have an apartment for rent.

W: Yes, I have. It's on the second floor. Would you like to have a look? Come this way, please.

Q: Who is the woman?

【解析】从四个选项看,该题提问的是身份职业。从对话中出现的关键词是an apartment for rent 和 ad.分析,录音中出现的男士和女士的关系应当是房东和租客的关系,因此这位女士应当是房东。

3. 数字计算题

【试题特点】

数字计算题常见的提问方式有:

What time...?

How far/long...?

How much/many...?

数字计算题一般涉及时间和价钱的运算。

(1)对活动发生时间的提问。在通常情况下,该类试题一般不会直接告诉我们问题中所问的时间,而是会涉及时间的一些简单的加减运算。要注意一些关键词,如:a quarter(to/past), half (past), daily, weekly, fortnight 等。

(2)商品的价格。同样,在短对话中,该类试题也涉及一些简单的加减乘除运算。要注意一些关键词,如:10% off, discount, double, half the price, couple, pair, dozen, a real bargain, on sale, change 等。尤其要注意单件商品的价格,买多件商品是否优惠、找零以及最后的问题是说话人要付的钱、单件商品的价格、还是买若干商品需要付的钱。

【答题技巧】

速记信息。这类题目的对话中一般都不会只出现一个数字,所以要对数字及相关要点信息进行速记。

听清问题。做这类题目时,必须清楚地抓住问题是针对什么提出,然后才能根据记录的信息将答案对号入座。

不要直取答案。这类题目的答案一般都不会是原文中数字信息的再现,往往需要经过简单的运算才能得出答案。

【典型例题】

【例3】A) $ 8.60.   B) $ 4.30.   C) $ 6.40.   D) $ 1.40.

W: Here's a ten-dollar bill. Give me two tickets for tonight's show, please.

M: Sure. Two tickets and here's a dollar forty cents in change.

Q: How much does one ticket cost?

【解析】在听对话的过程中需要对听到的几个数字进行速记:ten-dollar bill, two tickets, a dollar forty cents' change,通过对这几个数字的运算可以得到试题的正确答案B)。

Part IV Applied Writing

Resume(简历)

简历就是对个人学历、经历、特长、爱好及其他有关情况所作的简明扼要的书面介绍。简历是个人形象,包括资历与能力的书面表述,对于求职者而言,是必不可少的一种应用文。参加求职面试时,简历既能为介绍自己提供思路和基本素材,又能供主持面试者详细阅读。面试之后,还可以供对方存入计算机或归档备查。

Sample 1

Resume
Sandy Bright

2066 HONGAN BUILDING
NO. 233 JINTAI ROAD, BEIJING
PHONE: 13912345678
EMAIL: shen16900@sina.com

OBJECTIVE

A position that will further develop my strong marketing skills, and a training and counseling position with a business firm.

EXPERIENCE

Overseas Marketing Manager, PHE LO ADD Ltd., Singapore, 1999—present

Marketing Manager, G.S. STONE Ltd., Singapore, 1993—1999

Assistant Manager, Sony Music Co., Malaysia, 1988—1993

EDUCATION

Master of Business Administration, Boston University, 1990

Bachelor of Arts, Vocational Counseling, Virginia, Commonwealth University, Richmond, Virginia, 1982

COMPUTER OPERATING SKILLS

Macintosh; PageMaker, Word; WordPerfect, Excel and PowerPoint.

PERSONAL

Enjoy challenges and working with people.

Interested in increasing productivity.

Sample 2

Resume
Sandy Bright
65 Jones Rd EARLVILLE NSW 4444   0488 888 888(m)
j.sample@example.com

CAREER OBJECTIVE

   A position with an innovative, results-oriented firm where my excellent numerical, analytical and strategic thinking skills will be valued.

EDUCATION

1999—2001	Bachelor of Commerce Major in Accounting
	University of New South Wales
1998	Higher School Certificate

EMPLOYMENT

2000—2001	Accounts Assistant—Summer Vacation
	Bib and Bob Accountants
1999—2000	Sales Assistant—Part Time
	Value Supermarkets

KEY SKILL

   Communication; Teamwork; Numeracy

INTERESTS

   Soccer, chess, sculpture.

• *Unit 1   Job Hunting* •

REFERENCES

Professor Wu Sha
Head of School of Accounting   Manager Woolworths
University of New South Wales   Earlville Store
(contact details available on request)

Assignment: Suppose you are Alice Wang. You would like to apply for the position of sales manager of ABC Company. Please write a resume for it.

Part V   Cultural Express

Job Hunting Tips

Network!

Think of the people you know—relatives, friends, professors, classmates, co-workers at summer jobs, and others. Make more of an effort to meet with people, and use these conversations to ask their advice, to make them aware of your job search, to learn more about their jobs or their organizations, and to get the names of others who might be useful in your job search.

Target your resume.

Make sure your resume is targeted to the employers who receive it. Make sure your resume is easy to read and the most important details stand out. Make more than one resume if you are applying to more than one industry.

Be prepared.

You should have a copy of your resume with you at all times. It is also a good idea to have fresh copies of your resume prepared in case you are called to an interview at the last minute.

Create a contact database.

Write down all the employers you contact, the date you sent your resume, any contact made, people you talk to, and notes about those contacts. Keep a notepad with you at all times—take notes as soon as you hear about an opportunity or when you leave an interview. Get into the habit of updating your database daily.

Make a "to do" list every day.

This will help you organize your list of priorities and keep you focused on finding that perfect job.

Try the buddy system.

Link up with a friend who is also job hunting. Arrange to speak weekly and report on accomplishments, best practices, and future plans.

Learn how to talk about yourself.

Throughout your job search, you will speak with many people at different levels. You must be comfortable having conversations about yourself with other people. Keep in mind that you never know who may end up being useful to your job hunt.

Prepare an elevator speech.

You never know who you'll meet in an elevator, in line at the coffee shop, or on the street. Know what your skills are and how to communicate them. You should be able to tell prospective employers and others you meet what you can offer. You should also be able to talk about how your skills relate to the industries that interest you.

Find out all there is to know about employers in your field.

Remain current on any issues or developments in the field, read trade journals or professional publications, and read the newspaper. It is extremely impressive during an interview if you know about the latest merger or takeover in the industry.

Practice for each interview.

Preparation is key to interviewing well. Friends, relatives, and career services counselors can help you formulate strong answers to questions you might not anticipate. Look at the list of possible questions on the interviewing section and prepare yourself.

Follow up with leads immediately.

If you find out about a position late in the day, call right then. Don't wait until the next day.

Stay confident.

Job hunting takes time and energy. Remain confident, but prepare yourself for challenges ahead. Don't get disgruntled if you are still looking for a job and it seems like everyone you know has an offer. Most students find their jobs after graduation.

拓展词汇

书面申请材料

resume 简历；CV(curriculum vitae) 简历；school transcripts 成绩单；reference 推荐；a letter of recommendation 推荐信；referee 推荐人；certificate 证书；diploma 学位证书；graduate certificate 毕业证书

工作

employment 工作；work experience 工作经验；work history 工作经历；entry-level work 初级工作；previous work 以前的工作；position 职位；job title 职位；second job 第二职业；promotion 提升

Unit 1 Job Hunting

工作要求

responsibility 职责；duty 职责；able to meet deadline 有能力在限期内完成工作；work under pressure 在压力下工作；pay attention to detail 细心；good cooperation skills 良好的合作能力；oral and written skills 口头和笔头技能；team player (worker) 团队工作能力；communication skills 交流能力

面试常见问题

Tell us about yourself? 介绍一下你自己。
Tell me about your family or your girlfriend /boyfriend? 说说你的家庭或者你的女朋友/男朋友。
How do your friends describe you?
你的朋友如何描述你?
Why would you leave you last job and join our company? 为什么离开原来的公司而加入我们公司？
Why have you applied for this job?
你申请这份工作的理由是什么？
What is your understanding of the company?
你对本公司有哪些了解？
Why should we hire you? 我们为什么要雇用你?
Why are you the best person for this job?
你为什么是这份工作最佳人选？
What are your strengths and weaknesses?
你的强项和不足是什么？
Where do you see yourself in 5 years?
五年后的你将是什么样子？
What do you pride most in your life?
你生活中最引以为豪的事情是什么？
What's your biggest failure in your life?
你生活中最大的失败是什么？
How do you handle your conflict with your colleagues at work? 你如何处理和同事之间的冲突？
How do you work under pressure /stress?
你如何在压力下工作？

Unit 2

Interesting Jobs

Learning Objectives:

You are able to:
☞ Comment on different jobs
☞ Write a business contract

You are suggested to:
☞ Recognize the English expressions of different jobs
☞ Be familiar with some famous corporations

Unit 2 Interesting Jobs

Part I Listening and Speaking

Warm-up

Task 1

Directions: Can you tell what they do for a living? Please describe the people in the pictures.

| nurse | farmer | architect | teacher |
| photographer | worker | doctor | lawyer |

(1) (2) (3) (4)

(5) (6) (7) (8)

Task 2

Directions: Can you name some jobs in English? Work with your partner and match the following Chinese phrases with their English equivalents.

采购经理 ☆
首席执行官/总经理 ☆
仓库管理员 ☆
市场/营销主管 ☆
市场分析/调研人员 ☆
外贸/贸易经理/主管 ☆
财务/会计助理 ☆
报关员 ☆

★ CEO/GM/President
★ Marketing Supervisor
★ Market Analyst/ Research Analyst
★ Purchasing Manager
★ Warehouse Specialist
★ Trading Manager/Supervisor
★ Customs Specialist
★ Finance/Accounting Assistant

Oral Practice

Task 1

Directions: Read the dialogue and answer the following questions.

Talking About Career Choice

M: Have you thought about what you want to do, Betty?

W: Oh, yeah, Jack. I've been looking for jobs, I really want to start interviewing soon.

M: I've heard there're some good jobs in the government. They are pretty secure and offer excellent medical benefits.

W: Yeah, but those jobs seem so boring and the salaries are low. I'd prefer to find an interesting company to work for.

M: Well, what about something like sales work? You could be independent, creative...

W: Well, yeah, I really like the idea. I bet I could meet lots of different people and...

M: Sure!

W: ... do some traveling and maybe get out of the office...

M: Yeah, sounds nice! I wonder how much money you can make in sales, though.

W: Mm, I don't know... But, actually, I think I'd rather be on commission...

M: Really?

W: ... so that I'd get paid according to how successful I am.

M: Yes?

W: I could make much more money that way. I think I'd prefer that to getting a salary.

M: Well, I think you've got a great future in sales.

1. What would Betty really need to do before she gets a job?
   - ☐ to have an interview
   - ☐ to get help from Jack
2. What job does Jack suggest?
   - ☐ sales work
   - ☐ jobs in the government
3. What job does Betty prefer?
   - ☐ sales work
   - ☐ jobs in the government
4. What salary does Betty expect to get?
   - ☐ salary based on commission
   - ☐ salary only

Task 2

Directions: Suppose you are the manager of the Personnel Department of ABC Company. Your partner is a new employee. Here is a table of positions. Please introduce the different departments and staff in your company to the new employee. Role-play a conversation with your partner. Then reverse roles.

Listening Practice

Task 1

Directions: Listen to the dialogue, and tick (√) in the box at the end of the correct answer.

1. What job does Susan apply for?
    A. The job of a sales representative. □
    B. The job of a sales manager. □
    C. The job of a company representative. □
2. How many years of work experience does Susan have?
    A. One year. □
    B. Two years. □
    C. Three years. □
3. Does Susan have to work on Saturdays?
    A. Yes, she does. □
    B. No, she doesn't. □
    C. It is not mentioned. □

4. How long will the training last?
   A. Two weeks. □
   B. Three weeks.. □
   C. Four weeks. □
5. When will Susan know the result of the job interview?
   A. In about one week. □
   B. In about two weeks. □
   C. In about three weeks. □

Task 2

Directions: In this section you will hear a recorded short passage. The passage will be read three times. You are required to put the missing words or phrases in the numbered blanks according to what you hear.

How would you like a (1) _____ that can take you from the Eiffel Tower to the Caribbean to the Far East and back again? Or how about a (2) _____ that grants free air travel to you and your friends or family? Working in the (3) _____ industry can give you all this in what many find to be a fun and rewarding (4) _____. The airline industry is an important one around the world because people both need and want to (5) _____. In some areas of airline jobs, there is currently a (6) _____ in such areas as air traffic control and airport security. The Bureau of Labor Statistics is expecting this industry to (7) _____ considerably in the next few years as the (8) _____ gets better and more people are willing to travel. If you are willing to work while you are having fun, there are also (9) _____ for advancement in most aviation industry jobs, as well as the possibility of being transferred to other (10) _____.

Task 3

Directions: Listen to the conversation and work in pairs to decide whether the following statements are true or false according to what you have heard. Write "T" if the statement is true and "F" if it is false.

_____ 1. The last job Alice introduced to Frank was fairly good.
_____ 2. Alice thinks Frank is qualified for this job.
_____ 3. The company pays a basic salary and a high bonus.
_____ 4. The company wants college graduates with two years marketing experience.
_____ 5. Frank is not interested in the job at all.

Part II Reading

Text A

Before Reading:

1. Are you familiar with the following pictures?
2. Do you know what should be prepared before the wedding?

Event Planning: Wedding

Event planning is a relatively new career field. There are now courses that help people who are trying to break into the field. There must be training for an event planner to handle all the pressure and work efficiently. This career deals with a lot of communication and organization aspects. There are many different names for an event planner such as a conference coordinator, a special event coordinator, and a meeting manager.

Event planners' work is considered either stressful or energizing. This line of work is also considered fast-paced and demanding. Planners face deadlines and communicating with many people at one time. Planners spend most of their time in offices, but when meeting with clients the work is usually on-site at the location where the event is taking place. Some physical activity is required such as carrying boxes of materials and decorations or supplies needed for the event. Also, long working hours can be a part of the job. The day the event is taking place could start as early as

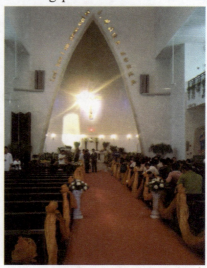

5:00 a.m., and then the planner may work until midnight. Working on weekends is sometimes required, which is when many events take place.

Weddings are significant events in people's lives and therefore, couples are often willing to spend considerable sums of money to ensure their wedding is organized as perfectly as possible. A wedding planner is a professional who assists with the design, planning and management of a client's wedding. Professional wedding planners exist throughout the world, most notably in the USA, UK and Western Europe. There are various wedding planning courses available to those who wish to pursue the career.

Wedding planners are often used by couples who work long hours and have little spare time available for sourcing and managing wedding venues and wedding suppliers. Planners are also popular with couples planning a destination wedding, where the documentation and paperwork can be complicated. Any country where a wedding is held requires different procedures depending on the nationality of the bride and the groom.

The services of a wedding planner can include:

- Interviewing the couple and the parents to identify their needs;

- Budget preparation;
- Planning a detailed checklist (from about a year in advance to a few days after the wedding);
- Guest list preparation;
- Arrangement of event venues (hotels, wedding manor, etc.);
- Identifying and hiring of wedding professionals and service providers (caterers, photographers, beautician, florists, bakers, etc.), and preparation and execution of contracts;
- Coordination of deliveries and services on the wedding day;
- Have a back-up plan in the event of a disaster;
- Assist and prepare legal documentation and translations—especially for destination weddings.

(543 words)

Unit 2　Interesting Jobs

New Words

（标★为A级词汇，标☆为超纲词汇）

coordinator	/kəʊˈɔːdɪneɪtə/	n.	协调者；同等的人(或物)
stressful	/ˈstresfʊl, -f(ə)l/	adj.	有压力的
★energize	/ˈenədʒʌɪz/	vt.	加强，给……以活力；使活跃；使充满热情
fast-paced		adj.	快步调的，快节奏的
deadline	/ˈdedlʌɪn/	n.	最后期限；截止期限；死线；原稿截止时间
decoration	/dekəˈreɪʃ(ə)n/	n.	装饰，装潢；装饰品；装饰图案，装饰风格；奖章
considerable	/kənˈsɪd(ə)rəb(ə)l/	adj.	相当大(或多)的；该注意的，应考虑的
★professional	/prəˈfeʃ(ə)n(ə)l/	n.	专业人士
venue	/ˈvenjuː/	n.	犯罪地点，案发地点；会场；(尤指)体育比赛场所
documentation	/ˌdɒkjʊmenˈteɪʃ(ə)n/	n.	证明某事属实的证据；记录；参考资料；文献的编集，文件分类
nationality	/naʃəˈnalɪti/	n.	国籍；国家
checklist	/ˈtʃeklɪst/	n.	清单；检查表；备忘录；目录册
☆manor	/ˈmanə/	n.	庄园；领地；庄园大厦；庄园主的住宅
caterer	/ˈkeɪtərə/	n.	(尤指职业的)酒席承办人，提供饮食及服务的人；筹办者
beautician	/bjuːˈtɪʃ(ə)n/	n.	美容师
florist	/ˈflɒrɪst/	n.	花商，花农，花卉研究者
baker	/ˈbeɪkə/	n.	面包师；烤炉；
★execution	/ˌeksɪˈkjuːʃ(ə)n/	n.	实行，履行，执行，贯彻；作成，完成
contract	/ˈkɒntrakt/	n.	契约；婚约；[法]契约法；行贿
★delivery	/dɪˈlɪv(ə)ri/	n.	传送，投递
back-up			备份

Phrases and Expressions

Event planning　　　　　　(婚礼)事务策划

Exercises

I. Reading Comprehension

Directions: Circle the right answer for the following questions.

1. Which one is not true about event planning?
    A. It needs a lot of communication and organization.
    B. It is a career field which has developed for a long time.
    C. The people who work on it must be trained to handle all the work.
    D. The people who work on it can be called an event coordinator.
2. What is an event planner?
    A. They almost stay in offices to handle all the work.
    B. They have to work on weekends.
    C. Their work needs communication with many people.
    D. Their work is an easy job without pressure.
3. Which one is true about wedding planning?
    A. It often exists in some developed countries, like USA, UK.
    B. It refers to the organization and management of a wedding.
    C. It is very helpful for the couples who have lots of spare time.
    D. It has one course to train people who want to work on it.
4. The right time for planning detailed checklist should begin from_____.
    A. a few days before wedding   B. a few years before wedding
    C. one month before wedding   D. one year before wedding
5. Which is not the service provided in a wedding?
    A. photographing   B. delivery   C. baking   D. washing

II. Word Usage

Directions: Complete each of the following sentences with the correct form of the italicized word given in the brackets.

1. She's very good at coping with _____ *(stressful)* situations.
2. He made a successful _____ *(career)* in business.
3. Everything has two contradictory _____ *(aspect)*.
4. I'm very _____ *(organize)* and extremely capable.
5. These snakes can be _____ *(identify)* readily
6. _____ *(prepare)* for the wedding takes very much time and money.
7. No _____ *(profession)* participated in the contest.
8. What _____ *(course)* have you completed?
9. Gambling is not _____ *(legal)* here.
10. All _____ *(event)* have proved our appraisal correct.

III. Blank Filling

Directions: Translate the Chinese part of the following sentences with the correct form of the words and expressions in the box.

| coordinate | decoration | deadline | professional | documentation |
| execution | delivery | venue | energize | client |

1. I hope we can finish this work before the _____. (最后期限)
2. Finally, ensure that you bring the required _____ with you. (文件)
3. She picked a large bunch of flowers for table _____. (装饰)
4. Decision-making is therefore slow, but _____ is rapid and single-minded. (执行)
5. You must _____ what you said with what you did. (与……一致)
6. Could you update us on the date, _____ and agenda items? (地点)
7. She can't come to the telephone; she's serving a _____. (顾客)
8. I need a _____ to sort out my finances. (专业人士)
9. It is one of the best ways to _____ your brain. (充满能量)
10. The strike caused a great delay in the _____ of the mail. (投递)

IV. Translation

Directions: Put the following English sentences into Chinese.

1. Couples who are very busy sometimes hire a wedding planner to help them with their preparations.
2. Budget cutbacks forced the company to let go of several employees.
3. They celebrate their wedding anniversary annually.
4. Emphasis on teamwork, good communication and coordination ability and organizational capacity.
5. A big wedding need special clothing, flowers, food preparation, photographs and music.

V. True or False

Directions: Decide whether the following statements are true or false according to the text. Write "T" if the statement is true and "F" if it is false.

_____ 1. Event planners should finish their work before a certain time.
_____ 2. Event planners don't need to do some physical activities.
_____ 3. The guest list is prepared by the couples and the parents.
_____ 4. It is necessary to prepare two plans for the wedding event.
_____ 5. There is no document and paperwork for a wedding planning.

Text B

Before Reading:

1. What is your image of "Mr. Right" or "Miss Right"?
2. What do you think is important in a successful marriage?

Premarital Counseling

What is premarital counseling and is it worth the time and money? It has been well documented that since the mid 1980s, 50 % of all marriages in the US result in divorce. Interestingly, it is the seventh year of marriage which presents itself as the most popular time to say goodbye. The latter statistic most likely gave rise to the cliché we all know these days as "the seven year itch".

After hearing these statistics, one cannot help but wonder, what does keep a couple together? What commonalities do successful marriages share? Research has proven that certain qualities will produce a successful marriage, including: high income level, compatibility, communication and conflict resolution skills as well as religious involvement. Evidence of the most common contributing factors to divorce include: marrying at a young age, poverty, and a low education level. Research shows that premarital counseling reduces the risk of divorce by up to 30%.

Truth be told, marriage is not only a beautiful love fest but also a living breathing partnership. There is love to grow, bills to pay, children to rear, dinners to prepare, a home to maintain, diapers to change, lunches to be made, social responsibilities to attend to... and on and on. A well-established partnership is required to successfully manage the family.

A lot of married couples admit that the real stresses arrive after the first child is born. Enter the first child and that is traditionally when life as it has been known shifts dramatically—the marriage gets hectic and life becomes a balancing act. Anyone that has kids is well aware of how un-sexy a new parent will feel at the end of the day; it is not uncommon at this point for the marriage to be pushed to the back burner. Premarital counseling offers the opportunity for a couple to discuss changes and stressful moments that may surface throughout a marriage. In premarital counseling, couples discuss topics such as child rearing, finances, life goals and work out any issues that may surface as a result of different philosophies. Premarital counseling allows a couple to start the marriage off, communicating about conflict and feelings. Supporters of premarital counseling claim that premarital counseling is proactive in that it prevents negative relationship habits from forming.

While premarital counseling may be a growing trend for couples in the 21st century, it is commonplace for Catholics to undergo a form of premarital counseling before marriage. Pre-Cana is the course all Catholic couples must undergo before they can be married in a Catholic church. Research has revealed that amongst religious groups, Catholics have the lowest divorce rate, whether or not this fact is a result of mandatory Pre-Cana is to be determined.

One could argue successfully that what ultimately keeps a couple together is questionable and reliant on many determining factors. However, premarital counseling will offer a couple opportunities that will better prepare them for challenges before them. As mentioned above, a couple has a 50/50 chance of remaining married throughout their lives. With odds like those, opting for premarital counseling makes a lot of sense.

(515words)

New Words

（标★为A级词汇，标☆为超纲词汇）

☆premarital	/priːˈmarɪt(ə)l/	n.	婚前
★counseling	/ˈkaʊns(ə)lɪŋ/	n.	咨询
document	/ˈdɒkjʊm(ə)nt/	n.	文件
divorce	/dɪˈvɔːs/	n.	离婚
★statistic	/stəˈtɪstɪk/	adj.	统计的
cliché	/kliːʃeɪ/	n.	陈词滥调
★compatibility	/kəmˌpatɪˈbɪlɪti/	n.	适合
rear	/rɪə/	v.	养育
☆hectic	/ˈhɛktɪk/	adj.	忙乱的
proactive	/prəʊˈaktɪv/	adj.	积极主动的
☆amongst	/əˈmʌŋst/	prep.	在……之内
Catholic	/ˈkaθ(ə)lɪk/	n.	天主教徒
mandatory	/ˈmandət(ə)ri/	adj.	强制的；命令的；义务的

Phrases and Expressions

premarital counseling	婚前咨询
the seven year itch	七年之痒

Exercises

I. Summary

Directions: Fill in the blanks with the appropriate words according to your understanding.

Premarital counseling is a very useful way to reduce the risk of (1)_____ . It is researched that a good (2)_____ is a well established (3)_____ of the couples. The real pressures and (4)_____ in daily life will bring some problems to the couples. Premarital counseling can help couples to (5)_____ changes and stressful moments. It is proactive in that it (6)_____ forming negative relationship habits. (7)_____ are common to have a form of premarital counseling (8)_____ marriage and they have the lowest divorce (9)_____ . Generally speaking, premarital counseling is a good method for couples to prepare for (10)_____ in their marriage.

II. Reading Comprehension

Directions: Circle the right answer for the following questions according to the text.

1. Which statement is true?
   A. It is documented that the US had a high divorce rate since 1980s.
   B. Most of the couples get divorced in their seventh year.
   C. Premarital counseling can stem the risk of divorce.
   D. There are lots of trifles in real life after the wedding.
2. The qualities which produce a good marriage do not conclude _____.
   A. compatibility   B. high income   C. young age   D. communication
3. Which is not the stressful moment in real life?
   A. pay the bills   B. prepare the meals   C. earn more money   D. play with the babies
4. Premarital counseling can help couples _____.
   A. rear their children   B. solve financial problems
   C. communicate feelings   D. form positive habits
5. What is Pre-Cana?
   A. It is used to reduce the divorce rate of all couples.
   B. It is a form of premarital counseling for Catholics.
   C. It is a course for all couples undergoing before marriage.
   D. It is the only reason that Catholics have the lowest divorce rate.

III. Vocabulary & Structures

Directions: Fill in the blanks with the proper expressions in the box.

| counsel | statistics | commonality | divorce | proactive |
| undergo | mandatory | odd | opt | questionable |

1. Couples may agree to _____ each other after a separation.
2. The explorers had to _____ much suffering.
3. Their motives for undertaking this study are highly _____.
4. She looks a bit _____. I wonder what has happened to her.
5. Attendance is _____ at all meetings.
6. Be _____ and start a conversation your partner prefers to speak.
7. They _____ for more holiday instead of more pay.
8. _____ suggest(s) that the population of this country will be double in ten years' time.
9. He refused to listen to the old man's _____.
10. That _____ helps make the trips even more special.

IV. Translation

Directions: Put the following English sentences into Chinese.

1. Don't rush into marriage; you might regret it later.
2. A happy home life needs the efforts from both sides of the couple.

3. Recently a lot of couples have been attending marriage counseling.
4. Communication, of course, doesn't need to be in words.
5. My duty to my family lies before my own interests.

Part III Strategies

词汇解析

词汇部分历来是考试的一个重点,这部分共20题,分为10道单项选择题和10道选词填空题两个部分。

一、解释参照法:利用句中的释义推导

此种方法的依据是词是对另一部分词汇意思的解释。

1. The medicine is for sale everywhere. You can get it at _____ chemist's.
   A) each   B) some   C) certain   D) any

正确选项为D)。本题中前一句中的everywhere就决定了第二句中的空格处填(at) any (chemist's)。

2. The manager spoke highly of _____ such as loyalty, courage and truthfulness shown by his employees.
   A) virtues   B) features   C) properties   D) characteristics

正确选项为A)。本句中as后面的名词loyalty(忠诚), courage(勇气) and truthfulness(实事求是)是对空格处名词进行的解释。本句中的三个名词归纳起来都属于人应当具有的"美德",所以本题的答案为A)。

3. I hope that you'll be more careful in typing the letter. Don't _____ anything.
   A) lack   B) withdraw   C) omit   D) leak

正确选项为C)。前边的 I hope that you'll be more careful 决定的后边的要填C)项omit, 意思是"遗漏"。

二、因果参照法:利用句中的因果关系推导

这种方法的依据是题干中的分句之间存在的因果关系。

1. Some old people don't like pop songs because they can't _____ so much noise.
   A) resist   B) sustain   C) tolerate   D) undergo

正确选项为C)。本句从don't like..., 推出后边的can't tolerate, 表示"不能容忍"的意思。

2. The poetry of Ezra Pound is sometimes difficult to understand because it contains so

many _____ references.

  A) obscure   B) acute   C) notable   D) objective

正确选项为A)。通过结果"difficult to understand"推出正确项"obscure",意思是"含糊难解的"。其他三个选项的意思分别是:B)敏锐,剧烈的;C)显著的,明显的;D)客观的。

3. Being somewhat short sighted, she had the habit of _____ at people.

  A) glancing   B) peering   C) staring   D) scanning

正确选项为C)。通过原因"short sighted"推出正确选项C) staring,意思是"凝视,盯着"。

4. Since the matter was extremely _____, we dealt with it immediately.

  A) tough   B) tense   C) urgent   D) instant

正确选项为C)。后半句中的副词"immediately"可以推出前半句的"urgent"(迫切的,紧急的)。

5. The shy girl felt _____ and uncomfortable when she could not answer her teacher's questions.

  A) amazed   B) awkward   C) curious   D) amused

正确选项为B)。句中and后边的uncomfortable是空白处所填入词的近义词,所给四个选项中只有awkward(尴尬的,难堪的)与uncomfortable意思相近。

三、转折参照法:利用句中的转折关系推导

这种方法的依据是题干中存在的转折关系。做题时可以通过转折词来确定选项,也可以通过句中词来确定选项中的转折词。

1. Even though he was guilty, the _____ judge did not send him to prison.

  A) merciful   B) impartial   C) conscientious   D) conspicuous

正确选项为A)。有罪而没有被判刑,表明法官是一个"仁慈"的人。所以A)项正确。其他三项的意思分别是:B)正直的、公正的;C)有良心的;D)显著的。

2. _____ their differences, the couple were developing an obvious and genuine affection for each other.

  A) But for   B) For all   C) Above all   D) Except for

正确选项为B)。句中的their differences, obvious and genuine affection可确定选项中的转折词只能是for all,意思是"尽管"。

3. Most nurses are women but in the higher ranks of the medical profession women are in a _____.

  A) scarcity   B) minority   C) minimum   D) shortage

正确选项为B)。通过most...but...可确定本题的正确选项为B),与most相对,表达"少数"的意思。

四、对比比较参照法：利用句中的反义或对比推导

此种方法是通过句中的转折词、反义词或对比词来确定选项。

1. These goods are _____ for export, though a few of them may be sold on the home market.

    A) essentially   B) completely   C) necessarily   D) remarkably

正确选项为A)。通过转折词though和对比词export与home market以及a few可确定选项为A)，意思是"基本上"。其他三项都不符合句意。

2. Mr. Morgan can be very sad _____, though in public he is extremely cheerful.

    A) by himself   B) in person   C) in private   D) as individual

正确选项为C)。通过后半句的转折词though和对比词in public...cheerful来确定sad in private，意思是"私下里"。

3. Why should anyone want to read _____ of books by great authors when the real pleasure comes from reading the originals?

    A) themes   B) insights   C) digests   D) leaflets

正确选项为C)。这里originals（原著）与空格处的词相对，所以空格处的词意思应当是"文摘，摘录"，显然，只有C)项为正确选择。

4. I think she hurt my feelings _____ rather than by accident as she claimed.

    A) virtually   B) deliberately   C) literally   D) appropriately

正确选项为B)。ranther than表明了by accident与空格处意思相对。by accident的意思是"偶然地，不经意地"，与此相对的应当是deliberately，"故意地"。

五、语意环境参照法：利用句中的语意环境推导

这里指的是纯粹根据题干的上下文来确定选项，也就是说选项的意义来确定正确选项。

1. The new appointment of our president _____ from the very beginning of next semester.

    A) takes effect   B) takes part   C) takes place   D) takes turns

正确选项为A)。四个选项的意思分别为：A)生效；B)参加；C)发生；D)轮流。从本句句意来看，只有A)项符合句意，本句大意是：对新校长的任命从下学期伊始生效。

2. Finding a job in such a big company has always been _____ his wildest dreams.

    A) under   B) over   C) above   D) beyond

正确选项为D)。一般来说能在一个大公司里谋到一份差事很不容易，所以她"超出了"一般人的梦想，所以只能选D) beyond，表示"超出……之外"的意思。

六、利用动词词组中的介词或副词确定正确选项

命题人员想考查考生是否掌握了某一动词词组的用法，在设计四个选项时，有时会把一个动词出现在四个选项中，只是后边的介词或副词不一样。在做这一类题时，如果我们认识某一词组，根据自己的判断毫不犹豫地选择你认为是正确的选项。如果不认识或拿不准它们的意义，我们可以根据上下文并以动词后边的介词或副词进行推导，如下例：

1. Having decided to rent a flat, we _____ contacting all the accommodation agencies in the city.

　　A) set about　　　B) set down　　　C) set out　　　D) set up

　本题的答案为A）。本句前边说"已经决定租房,我们联系房屋中介商……"这里需要填"开始"的意思。从动词后的四个介词来说,只有about有表示"将来"（be about）的意思,所以A为正确答案。需顺便补充的是,set about这一结构中,about是介词,,需要用动词的ing形式。

2. One day I _____ a newspaper article about the retirement of an English professor at a nearby state college.

　　A) came across　　B) came about　　C) came after　　D) came at

　本题的答案为A）。由于文中有"One day"这一时间状语和下文的意思,如果大家知道come across 表示"（意外）碰到",那就毫不犹豫地选A）。但如果不知道come across有此意义,我们根据四个介词的基本意义也可以判断A）为正确答案（across 交叉、穿过,come across 碰巧读到）。

3. When he realized the police had spotted him, the man _____ the exit as quickly as possible.

　　A) made off　　　B) made for　　　C) made out　　　D) made up

　本题的答案为B）。这里空格处要填的是表示"走向"之意,这里只有"for"表示在同一水平线上"向……方向"。注意,句中有exit一词,表示the man是在一个建筑物内,所以不可能用out the exit（注意上下文）,而且out是一个副词,后面接名词时需要有介词of,所以正确选项是B）而不是C）。

七、利用动词词组中的动词确定选项

　有些题的四个选项中的介词或副词一样,而动词则不一样,这时我们就可以利用动词的区别来确定正确选项,如下例:

　If you _____ the bottle and cigarettes, you'll be much healthier.

　　A) take off　　　B) keep off　　　C) get off　　　D) set off

　本题答案为B）。keep 与off合在一起是"与……保持距离,远离……"的意思,根据句子的意思"如果你不喝酒（这里bottle是替代,以名词bottle代动词喝酒）、不吸咽,你就会更健康",正确选项为B）。

八、利用句中的语法结构与固定搭配推导

1. It is useful to be able to predict _____ the extent which a price change will affect supply and demand.

　　A) from　　　　B) with　　　　C) to　　　　D) for

　正确选项是C）。to the extent是固定搭配,which引导的定语从句修饰先行词extent,所以空格处应填入的介词为to.

38

2. You cannot be _____ careful when you drive a car.
   A) very   B) so   C) too   D) enough
   正确选项为C)。cannot...too是固定搭配，表示"再……也不为过，越……越好"的意思。

九、根据词的同现确定正确选择项

同现指同一些词有时会出现在同一个语义场中，即同时出现在一个句子中，这就成了我们答题的依据。

1. Remember that customers don't _____ about prices in that city.
   A) debate   B) consult   C) dispute   D) bargain
   正确选项是D)。空格后的名词price决定其前的动词用bargain，构成bargain about，意思是：就……讨价还价。

2. A _____ to this problem is expected to be found before long.
   A) result   B) response   C) settlement   D) solution
   正确选项是D)。只有solution（措施）才能和problem同时出现，表示"某一问题的解决措施"。

3. Over a third of the population was estimated to have no _____ to the health service.
   A) assessment   B) assignment   C) exception   D) access
   正确选项为D)。"have/gain access to"这一词组的意思是：有使用……的权利。其他三项均不能和have...to同时使用。

十、利用固定词组推导

这里包括两种，一种是四个选项本身就是固定词组，另一种情况是句中的前面或后面的词与选项构成固定词组。

1. The politician says he will _____ the welfare of the people.
   A) prey on   B) take on   C) get at   D) see to
   正确选项是D)。所给四个选项意思分别是：A)捕食，掠夺；B)从事，担任；C)到达，得到；D)注意，照料。可见只有D)项才符合题意。

2. When I said goodbye to her, she _____ the door.
   A) saw me at   B) set me off   C) sent me to   D) showed me to
   正确选项是D)。show sb. to the door意思是"把某人送到门口"，其他三项均不符合习惯表达法。

3. The car _____ halfway for no reason.
   A) broke off   B) broke down   C) broke up   D) broke out
   正确选项是B)。broke down的意思是"抛锚，出故障"，其他三项不符合题意。

4. The political future of the president is now hanging by a _____.
   A) thread   B) cord   C) string   D) rope
   正确选项为A)。hang by a thread是固定用法，意思是"千钧一发，处境危险"。

十一、根据常识选答案

有些试题表述的是一个常识性知识，只要我们了解该常识，问题就迎刃而解。

1. A person's calorie requirements vary _____ his life.
   A) across　　　　B) throughout　　　C) over　　　　D) within

此题正确选项应为B。本题描述的常识是：在人的生命过程中对热量的需求是不断变化的。

2. Floods cause billions of dollars worth of property damage _____.
   A) relatively　　　B) actually　　　C) annually　　　D) comparatively

正确选项为C）。从句意来看，空白处需要填入的应是一个表示时间的词，所给四个选项中只有C）项 annually 表示"每年"的意思。其他三项A）相对地；B）实际上；D）相比较而言，都不符合题意。

Part IV Applied Writing

Contract（合同）

合同是当事人或当事双方之间设立、变更、终止民事关系的协议。涉外商务合同按繁简不同，可以采取不同的书面形式，如正式合同（Contract）、协议书（Agreement）、确认书（Confirmation）、备忘录（Memorandum）、订单（Order）等等。一份正式的合同通常由以下几个部分组成：

一、合同名称（Title）

二、前文（Preamble）

一般包括订约日期和地点（Date and Place of Signing），合同当事人及其国籍、主要营业场所或住所（Signing Parties and Their Nationalities, Principal Place of Business or Residence Addresses），当事人合法依据（Each Party's Authority，如该公司是"按当地法律正式组织而存在的"/ A Corporation Duly Organized and Existing Under the Laws of XXX），订约缘由/说明条款（Recitals or Whereas Clause）。

三、正文（Body）

一般包括定义条款、基本条款和一般条款。

定义条款（Definition Clause）：对合同中重复出现的关键名词术语进行明确定义，给出明确解释。

四、结尾条款（Witness Clause）

一般包括份数、使用的文字和效力（Concluding Sentence）、签名（Signature）。

Unit 2 Interesting Jobs

Sample 1:

> 1. NAME OF COMMODITY AND SCOPE OF THE CONTRACT
> 2. PRICE
> 3. PAYMENT
> 4. PACKING
>
>   IN WITNESS WHEREOF, this contract has been executed effective as of the date first above written.
>
> | THE BUYER | THE SELLER |
> |---|---|
> | ABC Company | China Yunhai Tea Export Company |
> | By: Tom Smith | By: Wangfang |
> | Date: 7/12/12 | Date: 7/12/12 |

Sample 2

> Sales Contract
>
> The undersigned Seller and Buyer have agreed to close the following transactions according to the terms and conditions set forth as below:
>
> 1. Name, Specifications and Quality of Commodity:
> 2. Quantity:
> 3. Unit Price and Terms of Delivery:
>
> The terms FOB, CFR, or CIF shall be subject to the International Rules for the Interpretation of Trade Terms (INCOTERMS 2000) provided by International Chamber of Commerce (ICC) unless otherwise stipulated herein.
>
> 4. Total Amount:
> 5. More or Less: _____ ‰.
> 6. Time of Shipment:
>
> Within _____ days after receipt of L/C allowing transhipment and partial shipment.
>
> 7. Terms of Payment:
>
> By Confirmed, Irrevocable, Transferable and Divisible L/C (letter of credit) to be available by sight draft to reach the Seller before _____ and to remain valid for negotiation in China until _____ after the Time of Shipment. The L/C must specify that transshipment and partial shipments are allowed.
>
> The Buyer shall establish a Letter of Credit before the above-stipulated time, failing which, the Seller shall have the right to rescind this Contract upon the arrival of the notice at Buyer or to accept whole or part of this Contract non fulfilled by the Buyer, or to lodge a claim for the direct losses sustained, if any.

8. Packing:

9. Insurance:

Covering _____ Risks for _____ 110% of Invoice Value to be effected by the _____.

10. Quality/Quantity discrepancy:

In case of quality discrepancy, claim should be filed by the Buyer within 30 days after the arrival of the goods at port of destination, while for quantity discrepancy, claim should be filed by the Buyer within 15 days after the arrival of the goods at port of destination. It is understood that the Seller shall not be liable for any discrepancy of the goods shipped due to causes for which the Insurance Company, Shipping Company, other Transportation Organization or Post Office are liable.

11. The Seller shall not be held responsible for failure or delay in delivery of the entire lot or a portion of the goods under this Sales Contract in consequence of any Force Majeure incidents which might occur. Force Majeure as referred to in this contract means unforeseeable, unavoidable and insurmountable objective conditions.

12. Dispute Resolution:

Any dispute arising from or in connection with this Contract shall be submitted to China International Economic and Trade Arbitration Commission for arbitration which shall be trialed in Nanjing and conducted in accordance with the Commission's arbitration rules in effect at the time of applying for arbitration. The arbitral award is final and binding upon both parties.

13. Notices:

All notice shall be written in _____ and served to both parties by fax/e-mail/courier according to the following addresses. If any changes of the addresses occur, one party shall inform the other party of the change of address within _____ days after the change.

14. This Contract is executed in two counterparts each in Chinese and English, each of which shall be deemed equally authentic. This Contract is in _____ copies effective since being signed/sealed by both parties.

The Seller: The Buyer:

Assignment: *Suppose you are Eric Liu, a trade manager of a Tea company. You would like to sign a trade contract with ABC Company. Please write a contract.*

Part V Cultural Express

Trying Different Jobs vs. Taking a Long Term Career

There is a discussion about young people's career choices. After graduating from university, should young people take several different jobs before taking a long term career? From my point of view, it is not a bad thing to try different jobs when going out into the world. Wise people would benefit a lot from the significant experience of various occupations, and finally head for a successful career.

The most essential reason is that one can make better self-orientation after several jobs. Stepping out of the campus and plugging into the society, young people usually lose themselves. However, an accurate self-orientation is crucial in a career. Trying different jobs will help young people to be aware of their potentials and weakness clearly, and to find his or her own way to compete with others. Many successful people today had engaged in a variety of jobs before they reach their current position. It is a necessary process for one to know oneself, to enrich oneself and to mold oneself through a rich experience of different jobs.

Another advantage of trying different jobs is that it builds up a broad interpersonal relationships. Most of the jobs today require not only professional skills but also the collaboration of different specializations. The experience in your former jobs will teach you how to tackle with people from all walks of life. For instance, in a business, if you had a wide range of human relations, anyone you know in other company or other field may give you a hand, and the crucial information or support offered by them will lead your business to success. In a word, the wide range of people you encounter in various jobs will favor you a lot in your further career.

Admittedly, we cannot deny that beginning with a long term career may have some advantages. In a long term job, one could gain more specialized experience, and will not worry about cases such as losing the position build up in the former jobs. But all of these benefits have a prerequisite, which is one should really fit the job. In this case, trying different jobs first is no doubt a good way toward your most suitable job. It is even suggested that you can start trying different jobs since your college years, like taking various internships that you are interested in.

In conclusion, trying different jobs before taking a long term career is a wise choice. If you can devote yourself to every job and learn from whatever you do, you will develop at a rapid pace and find a promising career in the near future.

拓展词汇

公司部门

Head Office 总公司;Branch Office 分公司;Business Office 营业部;Personnel Department 人事部;Human Resources Department 人力资源部;General Affairs Department 总务部;General Accounting Department 财务部;Sales Department 销售部;International Department 国际部;Advertising Department 广告部;Planning Department 企划部;Research and Development Department (R&D) 研发部;Secretarial Pool 秘书室

公司职务

CEO/GM/President 首席执行官/总经理;Deputy GM/VP/Management Trainee 副总经理;Director 总监;Partner 合伙人;CEO/GM/President Assistant 总裁/总经理助理;Logistics Manager 物流经理;Logistics Supervisor 物流主管;Logistics Specialist/Assistant 物流专员/助理;Purchasing Manager 采购经理;Purchasing Supervisor 采购主管;Purchasing Specialist/Staff 采购员;Trading Manager/Supervisor 外贸/贸易经理/主管;Trading Specialist/Assistant 外贸/贸易专员/助理;Merchandiser Manager 业务跟单经理;Senior Merchandiser 高级业务跟单;Merchandiser 业务跟单;Assistant Merchandiser 助理业务跟单;Warehouse Manager 仓库经理/主管;Warehouse Specialist 仓库管理员;Distribution Manager/Supervisor 运输经理/主管;Customs Specialist 报关员;Documentation Specialist 单证员;Courier 快递员;Warehouse Stock Management 理货员;Creative Artist/Designer 文字/艺术设计人员;Marketing/Advertising Director/VP 市场/广告总监;Marketing Manager 市场/营销经理;Marketing Supervisor 市场/营销主管;Market Analyst/Research Analyst 市场分析/调研人员;CFO/Finance Director/VP 财务总监;Finance Manager 财务经理;Finance

Unit 2 Interesting Jobs

Supervisor 财务主管/总帐主管；Accounting Manager/Supervisor 会计经理/会计主管；Accountant / Accounting Trainee 会计；Cashier 出纳员；Finance/Accounting Assistant 财务/会计助理；Financial Analysis Manager/Supervisor 财务分析经理/主管；Financial Analyst 财务分析员

职场文具

Double Sided Adhesive Tape 双面胶；Double Sided Foam Tape 双面海绵胶；Batteries for Calculator 计算器电池；Eraser 橡皮擦；Glue 胶水；Hard Cover Book 硬皮抄（笔记本）；Hole Puncher- 2 hole 打孔机（2 孔）；Label 标签；Magazine Tray 杂志架；Marker 记号笔；Measure Tape 卷尺；Name card holder 名片夹；Plastic Eraser 塑胶橡皮擦；Post-it Pop-up Note 便签纸；Rechargeable Battery 充电电池；Ruler 12" 12 寸尺子；Self Adhesive Tape 透明胶；Sharpener 铅笔刀；Stapler 订书机；Staples 订书钉；Steel Ruler 12" 12 寸钢尺；Super Glue 2g 万能胶；Tag Needle 5"s (standard size) 标准回形针

Unit 3

Business on Campus

Learning Objectives:

You are able to :
- ☞ Talk about making money on campus
- ☞ Understand terms in the stock market
- ☞ Discuss about employment qualities
- ☞ Write a specification

You are suggested to:
- ☞ Recognize the English expressions of foreign trade
- ☞ Be familiar with the procedures to start business on campus

Unit 3 Business on Campus

Part I Listening and Speaking

Warm-up

Task 1

Directions: Do you know their Chinese meanings? Try to say something about them.

| CV   credit card   stock exchange   diploma degree   application letter
bear market   bull market   graduation ceremony   job-hunting |
| --- |

Task 2

Directions: Do you know any English terms in foreign trade? Work with your partner and match the following Chinese phrases with their English equivalents.

出口信贷 ☆   ★ CIF
商品倾销 ☆   ★ FOB
自由贸易区 ☆   ★ wholesale price
关税 ☆   ★ port of shipment
装运港 ☆   ★ customs duty
批发价 ☆   ★ free trade zone
离岸价 ☆   ★ dumping
到岸价 ☆   ★ export credit

Oral Practice

Task 1

Directions: Read the following dialogue and tick (√) in the box at the end of the correct answer.

You: When was your company founded?
GM: It was founded in 2009.
You: How many employees do you have?
GM: We have over 200 employees in all so far. 60% of them are college graduates.
You: What are your main products?
GM: We manufacture phone accessories.
You: What's your annual output?
GM: The annual output is about 20,000 pieces.
You: Are you developing any new products?
GM: Yes, we are developing a new type of phone charger.
You: How about your R&D department?
GM: We have 3 research labs with ten full-time engineers.

1. When was the company established?
   ☐ 2009.   ☐ 2012.
2. What product do they produce?
   ☐ Book.   ☐ Phone accessories.

Task 2

Directions: Suppose your company wants to expand the business, and create a new position, press officer. Read the following job descriptions and role-play a job interview with your partner. Then reverse roles of interviewee and interviewer.

PRESS OFFICER

($ 22,000 per year)

A leading oil company needs a press officer for its busy office. You should be:
1) Good at making appropriate phone conversations.
2) Excellent at writing reports.
3) Able to go on business trips at least three times a month.
4) Willing to work late several times a week.

Unit 3 Business on Campus

Listening Practice

Task 1

Directions: Listen to the dialogues and tick (√) in the box at the end of the correct answer.

1. How did the woman get to know the job vacancy?
    A. by listening to the radio ☐
    B. by reading advertisement ☐
    C. from her head ☐
2. The woman found the job_____ .
    A. easy to do ☐
    B. easy to get high salary ☐
    C. fit her in her job career. ☐
3. What has the woman been doing in South Korea?
    A. as a Secretary ☐
    B. as a teacher ☐
    C. as a student ☐
4. What was the woman asked to do in the end?
    A. She was asked to write according to the man's request. ☐
    B. She was asked to write according to the advertisement. ☐
    C. She was asked to wait for the phone call. ☐
5. The interview wouldn't begin until _____.
    A. her applications were well done. ☐
    B. her name appeared on the short list. ☐
    C. the department head finished signing his name on the applications ☐

Task 2

Directions: In this section you will hear a recorded short passage. The passage will be read three times. You are required to put the missing words or phrases in the numbered blanks according to what you hear.

   Ladies and Gentlemen,
   Welcome to you all. We are pleased to have you here to (1)_____ our company. Today, we will first (2)_____ you around our company, and then you will go and see our (3)_____ and research (4)_____ . The research center (5)_____ just a year ago. You may (6)_____ any questions you have during the visit. We will (7)_____ to make your visit (8)_____ and worthwhile.
   Again, I would like to (9)_____ a warmest welcome to all of you on (10)_____ of our company, and I hope that you will enjoy your stay here.

Task 3

Directions: Fill in the blanks while listening to the dialogue and then practise the dialogue in pairs.

> Credit Card Application Form
> Name of User: Mr./Mrs./Miss/Ms _____
> Telephone number: _____
> Profession: _____
> Address: _____
> Any Estate/house: _____ your own
> Car's Make: _____ Monthly Salary: _____
> Date: _____

Part II Reading

Text A

Before Reading:

1. Have you ever thought of starting your own business on campus?
2. Talk with your partner about the advantages and disadvantages of self-employment.

advantages	disadvantages

To Be the Next Millionaire

In the months leading up to his college graduation in June, Yang Fugang spent most of his days away from campus, managing an online store that sells cosmetics, shampoo and other goods he often buys from local factories. A year and a half ago, like most men in the world, Yang Fugang became bewildered whenever anyone talked about girls' cosmetics. Now he's making a living from them.

Today, his store on Taobao.com—China's fast-growing online shopping bazaar—has 14 employees, two warehouses and piles of cash.

"I never thought I could do this well," said Mr. Yang, 23, who earned $75,000 last year. "I started out selling yoga mats and now I'm selling a lot of makeup and cosmetics. The profit margins are higher."

Taobao fever has swept Mr. Yang's school, Yiwu Industrial and Commercial College, where administrators say a quarter of its 8,800 students now operate a Taobao shop, often from a dorm room. They were attracted by the idea of Internet selling, and decided to set up their own online shop, with the idea of developing it into a regional shopping site later.

Here in Yiwu, which claims to be the site of the world's biggest wholesale market, Taobao has started to change the look of Yiwu Industrial and Commercial College.

The school's vice dean, Jia Shaohua, points out an area designated as a start-up site for students seeking to get rich. He points to students taking orders by computer, packaging products, sorting inventory and taking photos of the items for display online, then adds, "Around the school now, there is a whole Taobao internet supply chain."

Every afternoon, even this summer, when the school should be relatively empty, one can hear the ripping sounds of tape being wrapped around boxes in a building that could pass for a United Parcel Service shipping terminal.

"The students don't need a lot of money," Mr. Jia said. "They just get orders and go find the items at local factories."

Mr. Yang, the cosmetics seller, has become a campus hero. He operates his own warehouses a few miles from the school, in the basements of a pair of residential buildings.

Standing in his crowded warehouse, near boxes of Neutrogena sun block, hairpins, toothbrushes and a wide assortment of cosmetics, Mr. Yang says business could not be better. "Soon, I'll reach $150,000 a month in sales," he said, flashing a big grin.

(455words)
Source: nytimes.com 2009-08-14

New Words

（标★为A级词汇，标☆为超纲词汇）

graduation	/ɡrædʒʊˈeɪʃ(ə)n, -djʊ-/	n.	毕业；毕业典礼；
campus	/ˈkæmpəs/	n.	（大学）校园；大学，大学生活；
warehouse	/ˈwɛːhaʊs/	n.	仓库；货栈；
★ margin	/ˈmɑːdʒɪn/	n.	边缘
industrial	/ɪnˈdʌstrɪəl/	adj.	工业的，产业的；
★ commercial	/kəˈmɜːʃ(ə)l/	adj.	商业的
administrator	/ədˈmɪnɪstreɪtə/	n.	管理人；行政官
wholesale	/ˈhəʊlseɪl/	n.	批发
designate	/ˈdɛzɪɡneɪt/	vt.	指定；指派；
★ chain	/tʃeɪn/	n.	链；束缚；枷锁；连锁；
★ terminal	/ˈtɜːmɪn(ə)l/	n.	终点
toothbrush	/ˈtuːθbrʌʃ/	n.	牙刷
grin	/ɡrɪn/	v.	露齿而笑，咧着嘴笑

Phrases and Expressions

set up	建立；准备；安排；引起
make a living	赚钱过活；营生；糊口谋生；谋生
a pair of	一对；一双
a wide assortment of	各种各样的

Exercises

I. Reading Comprehension

Directions: Circle the right answer for the following questions.

1. When did Mr. Yang start his business?
   A. He started his business when he was at college.
   B. He started his business after graduation.
   C. He started his business in high school.
   D. He has never started his business.

2. What products did he sell first?
   A. He sold cosmetics first.
   B. He sold yoga mats first.
   C. He sold both cosmetics and yoga products first.
   D. He sold food products first.

Unit 3 Business on Campus

3. Why does online business in Yi Wu become more popular?
   A. Yi Wu has become the site of the world's biggest wholesale market.
   B. Students in Yi Wu have better access to all kind of products.
   C. Students can learn the skills of online business from their classmates and teachers.
   D. All the above mentioned.
4. Which one of the following statements is right according to the school dean?
   A. It is difficult for students to find the items at local factories.
   B. It needs a lot of money to start an online business.
   C. Students do not have to get orders.
   D. A Taobao industrial chain has already formed on campus.
5. Students feel _____ of the growth of online business.
   A. confident   B. difficult   C. dangerous   D. impossible

II. Word Usage

Directions: Complete each of the following sentences with the correct form of the italicized word given in the brackets.

1. Thomas was cheerful and _____ *(help)*, and we soon became good friends.
2. The goods that you ordered ten days ago will _____ *(deliver)* to you tomorrow.
3. Gas prices are _____ *(high)* here than in other parts of the country.
4. The past decade has seen great economic _____ *(develop)* in this country.
5. If the engineer _____ *(come)* here yesterday, the problem would have been solved.
6. While this new law does not _____ *(direct)* affect the quality of work, it will greatly benefit employees.
7. Now many young people spend several hours a day _____ *(talk)* on a mobile phone.
8. In China, it is quite _____ *(nature)* for people to go back home for the Spring Festival.
9. The manager was surprised at the news when he _____ *(receive)* the phone call yesterday.
10. Advances in medical technology have made it possible for people _____ *(live)* longer.

III. Blank Filling

Directions: Translate the Chinese part of the following sentences with the correct form of the words and expressions in the box.

| graduation | set up | making a living | wholesale | profession |
| designate | wrap | warehouse | grin | skill |

1. He took up writing after _____.(毕业)。
2. He _____, delighted at the memory. (咧着嘴笑)
3. The two sides agreed to _____ a commission to investigate claims.(建立)
4. _____ is not that easy for young people.(生存)
5. I stored up the old furniture in the _____.(仓库)
6. You can _____ it up in paper. (包裹)

7. For _____, we offer products at low price.(批发)
8. Please _____ who is to remain.(指定)
9. If you learn _____, you will have a better future after graduation. (技巧)
10. His _____ is a doctor. (职业)

IV. Translation

Directions: Put the following English sentences into Chinese.

1. Everyone is attracted by beauty and beauty is powerful.
2. Because poor translation might lead up to a misunderstand betwee the two parties in a business talk, I became more and more anxious about it.
3. He points out they have more knowledge and better tools than his generation had.
4. Your financial outlook could not be better.
5. I suddenly had a dizzy spell and felt as if it was the end of the world.

V. True or False

Directions: Decide whether the following statements are true or false according to the text. Write "T" if the statement is true and "F" if it is false.

_____ 1. Mr.Yang knew everything about cosmetics when he started his business.
_____ 2. There are growing numbers of people operating online shops at TaoBao in Yi Wu.
_____ 3. Many students felt it was very difficult to find the items from factories.
_____ 4. School discourages students to start online business.
_____ 5. Mr.Yang ended up with failure in business.

Text B

Before Reading:

1. What is door to door selling? Use your own words to describe it.
2. How do you think about door-to- door selling on campus?

Unit 3 Business on Campus

Money Making Schemes

The move-in day is a good time to sell many products to college freshmen, from daily necessities to yearlong passes for tourist spots. The sales people are students from higher grades. They are allowed to enter dorm buildings and know how to pal up with their peers quickly. Many upperclassmen grab this time to make a fast buck, and more importantly, to acquire early experience in business.

Zeng Renhui, a smart salesperson in Hunan University of Science and Technology, put herself in the freshman's shoes and figured out a new way to sell the SIM (Subscriber Identity Module) cards. "When I was a freshman, I felt awkward when an upperclassman walked into my dorm and sold things to me," Zeng recalled. "It was impossible for me to build trust with the student in such a short time." Zeng is the administrator of one of the QQ groups of the freshmen in her university. She had been communicating with the freshmen for the whole summer vacation and thus had won their trust. She made full use of the social network she built online and promoted her SIM card business in the QQ group. Zeng has of course created a roaring trade.

Liu xidan, 19. As a fan of 21st Century a weekly magazine, Liu xidan from Northeast Normal University(东北师范大学) applied to be a campus sales agent for the Weekly and was employed as the team leader. Liu was freed from door-to-door sales, but she still had to deal with challenging situations. Freshmen constantly changed their minds. Frequently they asked for a refund, because of untrustworthy hearsay that people who sold newspapers were all thieves, or another lame excuse. Liu wasn't able to cancel the subscription after issuing the invoice. She was stressed. "You need to be calm, patient and resourceful," said Liu. She kept smiling when facing unfriendly freshmen and patiently shared her personal experiences of reading the Weekly. Liu also sent free sample papers to teachers, who could serve as a credible reference.

Xu Bingchuan is a sophomore at Shan'xi University of Science and Technology. He had an eye for items that would sell well. He chose to sell locks instead of phone cards and newspapers, because it was more difficult to persuade freshmen to pay a hundred to subscribe to a paper for a year, than to spend only several bucks on useful locks. At first, Xu patiently found topics to engage the freshmen in chitchats, having looked at tips online about getting close to the customers. But it didn't work well. He met with cold shoulders most of the time. Luckily, Xu had been prepared for the challenge. "My intention was to see how difficult it could be to set up a business," said Xu, who would like a job in marketing or sales after graduation.

Being thick-skinned is necessary for a successful salesperson. Xu held on and adjusted his strategies. He gradually discovered that it's better to be direct with your customers and promote goods from the very beginning.

"Freshmen nowadays are smart. They know your intention and hate hearing you beating about the bush," said Xu. "Being an armchair strategist doesn't work. This is a useful lesson." Source: 21st Century 2011-09-30

New Words

（标★为A级词汇，标☆为超纲词汇）

★scheme	/ski:m/	n.	计划，方案；体系
freshman	/'freʃmən/	n.	大学一年级新生；
necessity	/nɪ'sɛsɪti/	n.	需要；必然性；
buck	/bʌk/	n.	（美）钱，元；
★promote	/prə'məʊt/	v.	促销
★agent	/'eɪdʒ(ə)nt/	n.	代理人，代理商
lame	/leɪm/	adj.	跛足的；僵痛的；不完全的；
patient	/'peɪʃ(ə)nt/	adj.	耐心地；有毅力地
item	/'ʌɪtəm/	n.	条款，项目；
persuade	/pə'sweɪd/	vt.	说服，劝说；使某人相信；
★engage	/ɪn'geɪdʒ, en-/	v.	吸引或引起（注意、兴趣等）
strategy	/'stratɪdʒi/	n.	战略，策略
smart	/smɑ:t/	adj.	聪明的；巧妙的；
intention	/ɪn'tɛnʃ(ə)n/	n.	意图；目的；
hate	/heit/	vt.	憎恨；厌恶；遗憾
bush	/bʊʃ/	n.	灌木丛

Phrases and Expressions

pal up with	和……结成好友，和……结伙
instead of	（用……）代替……
figure out	解决；弄明白
serve as	充当，担任

Exercises

I. Summary

Directions: Fill in the blanks with the appropriate words according to your understanding.

The first day is a good time to sell many products to (1)_____, from daily necessities to yearlong passes for tourist spots. The sales people are students from (2)_____ . They are allowed to enter dorm buildings and know how to (3)_____ their peers quickly. Many upperclassmen grab this time to (4) _____, and more importantly, to acquire early experience in business. Some students sell (5)_____ .Some students sell (6)_____ . Xu, a student, thought the cheap products were easy to sell, like (7)_____. Being(8)_____ is necessary for a successful salesperson. Xu held on and adjusted his (9)_____. He gradually discovered that it's better to cut loose and promote goods from the very beginning. "Freshmen nowadays are smart. They know your (10)_____ and hate hearing you beating about the bush," said Xu. "Being an armchair strategist (纸上谈兵) does not work. This is a useful lesson."

II. Reading Comprehension

Directions: Fill in the blanks of the following two statements according to the text.

1. It was impossible for _____ to build trust with the upper-grade students in such a short time.
2. Zeng Renhui made full use of the _____ she built online and promoted her business on campus.

III. Vocabulary & Structures

Directions: Fill in the blanks with the proper expressions in the box.

allowed to	pal up with	figure out	build trust with
deal with	instead of	serve as	buck
grab	necessities		

1. People not only need the life _____, but also comfortable life.
2. You should _____ him. He is the man to be trusted
3. We make the best out of every _____ we have.
4. Ultimately, we need to _____ our clients through communication.
5. Beautiful photographs _____ an excellent source of inspiration for designers.
6. _____ trying to change him, change how you view him
7. So how do we _____ these new challenges?
8. I _____ a good strategy.
9. This gives us opportunity to _____ market share.
10. The child will not be _____ play outside.

IV. Translation

Directions: Put the following English sentences into Chinese.

1. She still stuck to her point of view no matter how hard I tried to persuade her
2. Work and life create stress for each of us.
3. Men engage in more high-risk activities than women.
4. He met with cold shoulders most of the time.
5. He beats about the bush for a half hour without coming to the point.

Part III Strategies

翻译解析

PRETCO(B)中的翻译题分为两大类：一是句子翻译题，二是短文翻译题。两种题型均是英译汉，其中句子翻译题是选择题，总共有四个选项，选出最恰当的选项，而其他三个选项根据正确性程度，分值为1.5分、1分和0分；短文翻译题是翻译一篇50字左右的英文段落，满分是12。做这类翻译题要注意句子中关键词、常用句型、固定搭配、习惯用语等，特别注意常用词的一词多义，忠实原文，要符合汉语表达习惯，并在形式、内容上做到统一。

要先理解，然后对照选项，细心选择并确定答案。

1. 被动句的翻译：

这类考题较多，对于被动时态翻译考题，考生应经常将被动结构变成主动结构，这样更符合汉语语言特点。同时也要注意一些常用被动句型。

【例】2010年6月实考题

Many good movies have been produced recently, but I still prefer to watch old movies because they are more interesting.

A) 人们对电影是有兴趣的，特别是对老片子，所以我主张放映老片子。
B) 近来拍了很多好的影片，既古老又饶有趣味，我觉得人人都喜欢看。
C) 近来制作了很多好影片，但是我还是喜欢老片，因为老片更有趣。
D) 很多好的影片是最近拍的，但我依然觉得过去拍的影片很有意思。

这段话是被动态的翻译，movie是被动态的主语，但是这句话其实省略了by people，在翻译过程中，把by people这样的动作执行者主语省略，将英文原句中的主语做宾语，所以这一题C是最准确答案。

【例】2009年12月实考题

It is widely accepted that the cultural industry has been one of the key industries in developed countries.

A) 发达国家广泛接受，文化是支撑国家工业发展的关键事业。
B) 发达国家已普遍接受，文化产业应看成一种关键性的事业。
C) 大家普遍接受，发达国家应把文化事业看成一种关键产业。
D) 人们普遍认为，文化产业已成为发达国家的一个支柱产业。

这句话中，it is widely accepted that是固定句型，翻译为"人们普遍认为"，cultural industry has been one of the key industries in developed countries，这句话中，时态是完成时态的被动句，所以最好的答案是D。相类似的句型还有 It is hoped/reported/said/believed/known that....等。

Unit 3 Business on Campus

2. 长句的翻译：

1. 分析句子主干：主语、谓语；确定句子种类：包括主语从句、宾语从句、定语从句、状语从句、同位语从句等。

2. 把握好谓语动词的特点，确定时态、语态、语气等。

【例】2009年6月实考题

Good managers can create an environment in which different opinions are valued and everyone works together for a common goal.

A) 大家一定要齐心协力地工作，创造一个良好的环境，发表各种不同看法。要做好经理。

B) 为了共同的目标，好经理应该尊重各种不同意思，与大家一起工作，创造良好的氛围。

C) 好经理能够创造一种氛围，让不同意见受到重视并且每个人都有为共同目标合作奋斗。

D) 为了共同的目标，好经理应该能够提出各种宝贵的意见，为大家创造良好的丁作氛围。

这句话中，解题关键要看出 in which different opinions are valued and everyone works together for a common goal 是定语从句修饰 environment，是说明经理要创造什么样的环境，是一个尊重不同意见和大家为共同目标共同努力的环境，所以最佳答案是C。

【例】2008年6月的翻译段落题目节选

Please take a few moments to complete our customer response form so that we may serve you better in the future.

译文：请抽出几分钟时间来填写反馈信息表，以便我们将来可以更好的为您服务。

这句 so that 表示目的，引导了目的状语从句。

3、注意句子中某些关键词、常用句型、固定搭配、习惯用语等。特别注意常用词的一词多义，尤其是要注意强调句、倒装句、省略句等。

【例】2010年6月实考题

If your company insists on your price, we will have to turn to other suppliers for the goods.

A) 假如贵公司要调整价格，请及早告知我们，以便另做安排。

B) 假如贵公司提高价格，我们不得不从其他地方另寻货源。

C) 如果贵公司不给折扣价，我们不得不采用其他方式购货。

D) 如果贵公司坚持你方报价，我方只能找其他供应商进货。

这句话中，解题关键要看出 turn to 和 insist 的意思，turn to sb. 是表示向某人寻求帮助，在这里是表示向别的公司进货，insist 是坚持的意思，所以最佳答案是D。

【例】2009年12月实考题

Not until this week were they aware of the problems with the air-conditioning units in the hotel rooms.

A) 这个星期旅馆里的空调间出问题了，他们没有意识到。

59

B) 直到这个星期他们才意识到该修理旅馆房间里的空调了。
C) 直到这个星期他们才知道旅馆房间里的空调设备有问题。
D) 他们查不出旅馆房间内空调的故障,这个星期会请人来检查。

这句话中,解题关键要看出这句是倒装句,not until 表示....直到....才,且否定词在句首,整句话部分倒装,这句话变成正句序是 They were not aware of the problem with the air-conditioning units in the hotel rooms until this week. 所以最佳答案是 C。

练习:

☐ All over the world men are searching for new techniques to provide a great deal of housing, inexpensive and quick, for millions of low and middle income families, and especially to meet the urgent housing needs caused by flood and earthquakes.

☐ A company in U.S.A. believes it has found one method, houses made of paper. About ten years ago the company supplied a number of the newest paper houses as urgent housing for thousands of farm workers in California. Today, the paper houses are still holding up well. The builders now guess that the houses will have a useful life of at least 15 or 20 years.

Part IV   Applied Writing

Specifications (说明书)

说明书,是以应用文体的方式对某事或物来进行相对的详细表述,使人认识、了解到某事或物。说明书要实事求是,不可为达到某种目的而夸大产品的作用和性能。说明书要全面地说明事物,不仅介绍其优点,同时还要清楚地说明应注意的事项和可能产生的问题。说明书可根据情况需要,使用图片、图表等多样的形式,以期达到最好的说明效果。

Sample 1: Read the following medicine specification.

> Easy Stomach Tablets Relieve Your Upset Stomach Quickly
> Indications: It is effective in the treatment of stomach ache resulted from too much eating or drinking
> Dosage: 1 tablet every six hours. Do not take more than 6 tablets in 24-hour period.
> Storage: Store in tightly sealed containers.
> Caution: Not recommended for children under 12 years.

• Unit 3 Business on Campus •

Sample 2: Read the following specification of Clean & Clear Correction Fluid.

> SHAKE WELL · TOUCH ON · DO NOT BRUSH
> Apply sparingly by dotting the outline of each letter with brush-tip
> Allow 8—10 seconds to dry. Recap tightly after each use
> Available in colors: white, black, blue
> Avoid contact with clothing. Wipe up accidental spills quickly
> Caution: The content can be toxic. Non-flammable

Specification Expressions and Sentence Structures

We recommend the user	……我们建议用户……
It can prolong the product life	………这可以延长产品使用寿命
Its clinical effects include	……临床效果包括……
(be) active/effective against	……对……有效地
In the treatment of all forms of disease	……治疗各种疾病……

Assignment: Suppose you are from a cell-phone company. Your company recently has developed a new cell-phone. Please write a short cell-phone specification.

Part V Cultural Express

Tips on Starting an E-Business

Starting an e-business can be a fast and cost-effective way to enter the marketplace and reach a growing pool of potential customers. According to the U.S. Census Bureau, American consumers are increasingly turning to the Internet to locate goods and services, having spent an estimated $133 billion online in 2008—a figure that accounted for 3.3 percent of total sales. Here are a few tips that can help your fledgling web presence turn into a profitable enterprise.

Choose a Strong Name

Choosing the right name for your company is one of the most important decisions you'll make when starting an e-business. Business names like Amazon and Yahoo! have little relation to the products and services offered by their respective companies, however, they share a few common properties: they are short, easy to remember and easy to spell. Those three factors are critical to the success of any e-business, because customers must be able to quickly and easily find your company online. When choosing a name for your e-business, consider how it will look and sound as a domain name. Amazon.com is much easier to remember than Jeff Be zoz Online BookStore .com. Also remember that most customers are used to typing ".com". Domain names that end in ".net", ".biz" or other, lesser-known extensions can cause confusion and appear less trustworthy than their ".com" counterparts.

Invest in Your Website

Your e-business website will serve as your customers' only portal to your company's goods and services, so it's important to make sure that it looks professional and provides customers with the resources needed to research and make purchasing decisions about your products. The cost of hiring a professional web design firm to help you open your virtual doors will vary widely depending on your needs, but this is one area where pinching pennies will hamper your growth.

Just like a bricks-and-mortar storefront should be clean and welcoming, a virtual storefront should showcase a pleasing layout that highlights the most important information and makes navigation simple.

Get Verified

The anonymity of the Internet can hinder a customer's confidence in an unfamiliar company. There are, however, a number of third-party services that specialize in confirming that your e-business is more than just a fly-by-night operation.

Companies like McAfee, TRUSTe and Trust Guard verify your identity and business practices and, if you meet their requirements, provide "trust seals" that you can display on your website to help customers feel more secure about doing business with you. According to e-commerce specialist Dave Taylor, more than 70 percent of online consumers look for trust seals when doing business online.

There are three types of trust seals: security seals, which verify the security of your website and customer data; privacy seals, which certify that your business's privacy policy protects customer information; and identity seals, which certify that there is an identifiable human presence behind the online storefront.

拓展词汇

爱屋及乌 Love me, love my dog.
百闻不如一见 Seeing is believing.
比上不足，比下有余 Worse off than some, better off than many. To fall short of the best, but be better than the worst.
笨鸟先飞 A slow sparrow should make an early start.
不眠之夜 White night
不以物喜，不以己悲 Not pleased by external gains, not saddened by personal losses.

不遗余力 spare no effort; go all out; do one's best
不打不成交 No discord, no concord.
拆东墙补西墙 Rob Peter to pay Paul.
辞旧迎新 bid farewell to the old and usher in the new; ring out the old year and ring in the new
大事化小，小事化了 Try first to make their mistake sound less serious and then to reduce it to nothing at all.
大开眼界 open one's eyes; broaden one's horizon; be an eye-opener
国泰民安 The country flourishes and people live in peace
过犹不及 Going too far is as bad as not going far enough; beyond is as wrong as falling short; too much is as bad as too little
功夫不负有心人 Everything comes to him who waits.

Unit 4

Customer Service

Learning Objectives:

You are able to:

- Make or file a complaint
- Introduce after-sale service
- Understand and respond to customers' complaint
- Comment on customer service
- Write a complaint letter

You are suggested to:

- Identify the English expressions of complaint
- Know successful business strategies

Unit 4 Customer Service

Part I Listening and Speaking

Warm-up

Task 1

Directions: Choose the correct English name from the box for each of the following pictures.

| Customer Service Department | Cashier | Warehouse |
| Inquiry Desk | Delivery Service | Reception Desk |

Task 2

Directions: Work with your partner and match the following Chinese names with the English equivalents.

总公司 ☆   ★ Executive Secretary
分公司 ☆   ★ Multinational Corporation
人事部 ☆   ★ Quality Control Department
总务部 ☆   ★ Purchasing Department
公共关系部 ☆   ★ Public Relations Department
采购部 ☆   ★ General Affairs Department
质检科 ☆   ★ Personnel Department
跨国公司 ☆   ★ Branch Office
行政秘书 ☆   ★ Head Office

Oral Practice

Task 1

Directions: Read the following short conversations between the visitor (V) and the receptionist (R) and then tell your partner what they are talking about and answer the following questions.

R: How may I help you?

V: Yes, I am James Mason from Anderson and Associates. I would like to see Mr. Smith.

R: Do you have an appointment?

V: Yes, he knows I am coming. Our meeting is set for 2 o'clock.

R: I wonder if Mr. Smith forgot your meeting, I am afraid he left the office this morning and he is not expected back until after 4 pm. Let me find out if he made an arrangement for someone else to meet with you in his place. Will you please have a seat?

V: Sure.

R: Yeah, Mr. Mason, I just checked with their office manager Ms. Terry, she said Mr. Smith briefed her on your project and she is just finishing up a meeting now. She should be with you shortly. Would you like me to show you around while you are waiting?

V: That would be very nice, thank you!

R: Right this way Mr. Mason, we can start with our front office, when Ms Terry is ready, you may take the elevator at the front to the 6th floor. There is a conference room already prepared.

1. When will the meeting be expected to be held?
   ☐ 2 o'clock.   ☐ 3 o'clock.
2. What is Ms. Terry's job?
   ☐ Office manager.   ☐ General manager.
3. Why does Ms. Terry meet Mr. Mason at last?
   ☐ Because Mr. Smith is out and asks Ms. Terry to discuss business with Mr. Mason.
   ☐ Because Ms. Terry is more suited to handle this case.

Task 2

Directions: Read the following conversations and find the themes based on the clues given below.

> hotel reception job   ask for direction
> explain the delivery service   ask if there is an access to the internet
> write a customer satisfaction survey

1. R: What can I do for you?
   V: I want to book a double room.
2. R: Hello, is there anything else that I can help you with?
   V: Yes, I am looking for the laundry room.
3. R: The products would be delivered within 2 days after you place your order.
   V: Ok. I will tell our manager about this.
4. R: If you have any problem, please don't hesitate to let me know.
   V: Thanks. Is there an access to the internet in the room?
5. R: Recently, we are doing a customer satisfaction survey, could you help us fill out the form?
   V: Sure, I'd love to.

Task 3

Directions: Suppose you want to buy a computer, you(Y) come to the shop and ask a shop assistant (A) about the computer and the after-sale service. Role-play a conversation with your partner. Then reverse the roles.

COMPUTER FOR SALE

1 year warranty

Free 24-hour delivery

14-day money back guarantee

180 RMB software package free

Buy now, only RMB 4999 !

For further information

Please call 6280110 or visit www. 4u.com.cn

Listening Practice

Task 1

Directions: Listen to the dialogue and tick (√) in the box at the end of the correct answer.

1. The woman welcomed the man to _____.
   A. rental Property Management ☐
   B. manager's office ☐
   C. the centre of Rental Property Management ☐
2. The specific location in the man's mind is _____.
   A. near the hospital ☐
   B. near the swimming pool ☐
   C. near the university ☐
3. The man would like to rent a two-bedroom apartment at the price from _____.
   A) $400 to $500 a month ☐
   B) $400 to $450 a month ☐
   C) $350 to $400 a month ☐
4. The man would like to have _____.
   A) a dishwasher and a swimming pool ☐
   B) a dishwasher, a bathroom and central air ☐
   C) a dishwasher, a washing machine and air conditioner ☐
5. What did the woman suggest the man to do?
   A) She needs a damage deposit of $300. ☐
   B) She needs the deposit of $300 as soon as possible. ☐
   C) She suggests the man look around Broadway. ☐

Task 2

Directions: In this section you will hear a recorded short passage. The passage will be read three times. You are required to put the missing words or phrases in the numbered blanks according to what you hear.

Ladies and gentlemen,

　　It's a great (1) _____ to have you visit us today. I'm very happy to have the (2) _____ to (3) _____ our company to you. The company was established in (4) _____. We mainly manufacture electronic goods and (5) _____ them all over the world. Our sales were about (6) _____ last year, and our business is growing steadily.

　　We have offices in Asia, (7) _____ and Europe. We have about 1,000 employees, who are actively working to serve the needs of our (8) _____. In order to further develop (9) _____ market, we need your help to promote (促销) our products.

　　I (10) _____ doing business with all of you.

　　Thank you.

Task 3

Directions: Listen to the conversation and work with your partner to fill in the form given below.

```
Gree Microwave Oven

Specifications:
Length:    40 cm
Width:     25 cm
Height:    20 cm
Material:  _____
Color:     _____
Shape:     rectangular

Manufacturer: Shenzhou Electronic, Ltd
Guarantee period: _____
```

Part II Reading

Text A

Before Reading:

Do you think customer service is important? Why?

The Greatest Customer Service Story Ever Told

The following story is fully true. Most importantly, this is AMAZING. When my alarm clock went off at 3:30 this morning, I knew it was going to be a long day. I was catching a 7:00 am flight out of Newark (纽瓦克) to Tampa (坦帕), Florida (佛罗里达), for a lunch meeting in Clearwater, then going back to Newark on a 5pm flight, arriving around 8:10 pm, and getting to my apartment by 9:00 pm or so. As a businessman we all have busy schedule like this.

I made my flight and got to my lunch meeting. My first meal of the day was that lunch. By the time I got back to the airport, it was close to 4:00 pm. Flight boarded at 4:30 pm, and I knew when I got home, I wouldn't have time to stop for dinner anywhere, and certainly didn't want to get fast food at either airport. When I got on the plane, my stomach was rumbling a bit, and I had visions of a steak in my head.

As I'm a steak lover, I go out of my way to try steakhouses all around the world when I can. Over the past few years, I've developed the liking for Morton's Steakhouses (莫顿牛排馆) and if I'm doing business in a city which has one, I'll try to plan a dinner there if I can. I'm a regular customer, and Morton's knows it. They have a spectacular Customer Relations Management (CRM) system in place, as well as a spectacular social media team, and they know when I call from my mobile number who I am, and that I eat at their restaurants regularly. Never underestimate the value of a good CRM system.

As we were about to take off, I made a joke and tweeted the following:

I certainly didn't expect anything from that Tweet. It is just an online joke.

I shut off my phone and we took off. Two and a half hours later, we landed at Newark airport. Walking off the plane, I headed towards the area where the drivers wait, as my assistant Meagan had reserved me a car home.

Looking for my driver, I saw my name, waved to him, and started walking towards the gate, like I had done hundreds of times before.

"Um, Mr. Shankman," he said, "There's a surprise for you here."

I turned around and saw the driver was standing next to someone else, who I just assumed was another driver. Then I noticed the "someone else" was in a tuxedo. And he was carrying a Morton's Steakhouse bag.

Alex, from Morton's Steakhouse walked up to me, introduced himself, and handed me a bag. He then told me that he'd heard I was hungry.

I opened the bag. Inside were a 24 oz. Porterhouse steak, an order of Colossal Shrimp, a side of potatoes, Morton's famous bread, two napkins, and silverware.

I was astonished!

@petershankman
Peter Shankman

Hey @Mortons - can you meet me at newark airport with a porterhouse when I land in two hours? K, thanks. :)

New Words

(标★为A级词汇,标☆为超纲词汇)

amazing	/əˈmeɪzɪŋ/	adj.	令人惊异的
board	/bɔːd/	v.	(火车、轮船、飞机等)接受乘客
rumble	/ˈrʌmb(ə)l/	v.	隆隆作响
★vision	/ˈvɪʒ(ə)n/	n.	幻影;想象力
liking	/ˈlaɪkɪŋ/	n.	嗜好
★regular	/ˈrɛgjʊlə/	adj.	经常地(regulate v. ; regulation n.)
spectacular	/spɛkˈtakjʊlə/	adj.	惊人的
☆underestimate	/ˌʌndərˈɛstɪmeɪt/	v.	低估
★assume	/əˈsjuːm/	v.	以为;假设
notice	/ˈnəʊtɪs/	v.	注意到
steakhouse	/ˈsteɪkhaʊs/	n.	牛排餐厅
napkin	/ˈnapkɪn/	n.	餐巾纸
silverware	/ˈsɪlvəwɛː/	n.	餐具
★astonish	/əˈstɒnɪʃ/	v.	使惊讶,使大为吃惊

Phrases and Expressions

take off	(飞机)起飞
headed towards	朝……方向走
next to	紧邻;在……近旁

Note

Tampa	坦帕
Florida	佛罗里达
Morton's Steakhouses	莫顿牛排馆,是美国一家有名的连锁餐厅。
Newark	纽瓦克,位于新泽西州
Clearwater	清水市,位于佛罗里达州
Porterhouse steak	上等腰肉牛排
an order of Colossal Shrimp	一份大虾

Exercises

I. Reading Comprehension

Directions: Circle the right answer for the following questions.

1. What does Mr. Shankman do for a living?
    A. He is a businessman.
    B. He is a chef.
    C. He likes traveling.
    D. He is very fond of steaks.
2. When was the flight to Newark boarded?
    A. 4:30 p.m.
    B. 5:30 p.m.
    C. 2:30 p.m.
    D. Not mentioned.
3. What can a Customer Relations Management (CRM) system do?
    A. A CRM system effectively ensures a better communication with customers.
    B. From a CRM system, a regular customer can get a better service.
    C. From a CRM system, the customer might also receive the similar good service in other cities.
    D. All of the above.
4. Which one of the following statements is correct according to the text?
    A. Mr. Shankman did not taste steak at last.
    B. Mr. Shankman thinks a CRM system is not so desirable.
    C. Morton's Steakhouses called Mr. Shankman and invited him to eat in their restaurant.
    D. Morton's Steakhouses delivered a delicious meal all the way to the airport.
5. It is _____ for Mr. Shankman to get a bag from Morton's Steakhouses at the airport.
    A. easy   B. difficult   C. surprising   D. impossible

II. Word Usage

Directions: Complete each of the following sentences with the correct form of the italicized word given in the brackets.

1. Nowadays, electronic _____ *(pay)* is a more convenient way to pay for purchases than cash and checks.
2. Most of the high school students who _____ *(interview)* yesterday believed that they should continue with their education.
3. According to the survey _____ *(conduct)* recently, 52% of American business people booked their business travel online last year.
4. The _____ *(grow)* of online shopping is producing a fundamental change in consumer behavior.
5. The total output of this factory _____ *(double)* since it was put into operation in 2006.
6. It is the _____ *(responsible)* of the Human Resources Department to employ new staff members.
7. It was reported that the _____ *(injure)* people were taken to the hospital immediately after the accident.

8. The bank refused _____ (accept) my application for the loan because they were not convinced by my business plan.
9. It's important to realize how _____ (quick) this disease can spread over the globe.
10. Of all the marketing plans proposed at the meeting, this one is believed to be the _____ (practical).

III. Blank Filling

Directions: Translate the Chinese part of the following sentences with the correct form of words and expressions in the box.

| amazing | liking | underestimate | take off | head towards |
| leave | regular | apply for | communicate | |

1. In our phone interview she told me her _____ story. (有趣的)
2. Certainly he shows little _____ for China and its culture. (喜欢)
3. If you want to retain youthful vigor, you have to take _____ exercise. (周期性的)
4. We must never _____ the power of these achievements. (低估)
5. As our plane _____, I told myself that I would absolutely return someday. (起飞)
6. He _____ the school. (走向)
7. Don't _____ pets in the room while you are out. (留下)
8. I want to _____ this job. (申请)
9. _____ is very important in interpersonal relations. (沟通)

IV. Translation

Directions: Put the following English sentences into Chinese.

1. We will land at Taibei Airport in ten minutes.
2. I want to reserve a single room with shower.
3. They assume customers know more than they do.
4. As you like music, you can introduce some famous singers to me.
5. Someone you know may give you a tip that leads you to an astonishing opportunity.

V. True or False

Directions: Decide whether the following statements are true or false according to the text. Write "T" if the statement is true and "F" if it is false.

_____ 1. Mr. Shankman did not like eating streak.
_____ 2. Mr. Shankman posted on the internet a message that he wanted to eat steak.
_____ 3. Morton's Steakhouses did not see this online message.
_____ 4. Morton's Steakhouses is famous for Chinese food.
_____ 5. Good customer service is very important in business.

Text B

Before Reading:

What is good customer service? Could you give some examples?

Rules for Good Customer Service

It's Good customer service that is the lifeblood of any business. You can offer promotions and low prices to bring in as many new customers as you want, but unless you can get some of those customers to come back, your business won't be profitable for long. Good customer service is all about bringing customers back, and about sending them away happy—happy enough to pass positive feedback about your business along to others, who may then try the product or service you offer for themselves and in turn become repeat customers. If you truly want to have good customer service, all you have to do is to ensure that your business consistently does these things:

Answer your phone. Hire staff if you need to. Make sure that someone is picking up the phone when someone calls your business. Not a fake "recorded robot".

Don't make promises unless you will keep them. If you say, "Your new bedroom furniture will be delivered on Tuesday," make sure it is delivered on Tuesday. Otherwise, don't say it. Think before you give any promise.

Listen to your customers. Is there anything more frustrating than telling someone what your problem is and then discovering that he hasn't been paying attention and needs to have it explained again? Let your customer talk and show him that you are listening by making the appropriate responses, such as suggesting how to solve the problem.

Deal with complaints. If you give the complaint your attention, you may be able to please this one person this one time. Position your business one customer at a time to earn the benefits of good customer service.

Be helpful—even if there's no immediate profit in it. The other day I went into a local watch shop because I had lost the small piece that clips the pieces of my watch band together. When I explained the problem, the owner said that he thought he might have one lying around. He found it, attached it to my watch band—and charged me nothing! Where do you think

I'll go when I need a new watch band or even a new watch? And how many people do you think I've told this story to?

Train your staff to be always helpful, courteous, and knowledgeable. Do it yourself or hire someone to train them. Talk to them about good customer service and what it is regularly. Most importantly, give every member of your staff enough information and power to make those small customer-pleasing decisions, so he never has to say, "I don't know, but so-and-so will be back at…"

Take the extra step. If someone walks into your store and asks you to help them find something, don't just say, "It's in Aisle 3". Lead the customer to the item. Better yet, wait and see if he has questions about it, or his further needs. They may not say anything to you at the moment, but when you make an extra effort they will tell other people.

Throw in something extra. Whether it's a coupon for a future discount, additional information on how to use the product, or a genuine smile, people love to get more than they expected

(531 words)

New Words

（标★为A级词汇，标☆为超纲词汇）

★promotion	/prə'məʊʃn/	n.	促销,提升,升级;（商品等的）推广
★positive	/'pɒzɪtɪv/	adj.	积极的;确实的
★feedback	/'fi:dbæk/	n.	反馈
promise	/'prɒmɪs/	n.	允诺,许诺
★deliver	/dɪ'lɪvə/	v.	投递;传送 (delivery n.)
appropriate	/ə'prəʊprɪət/	adj.	适当的;恰当的
immediate	/ɪ'mi:dɪət/	adj.	立即
profit	/'prɒfɪt/	n.	收益,得益;利润
★courteous	/'kɜ:tjəs/	adj.	有礼貌的;谦恭的
knowledgeable	/'nɒlɪdʒəb(ə)l/	adj.	了解全面情况的;知识渊博的
☆aisle	/aɪl/	n.	过道,通道
moment	/'məʊm(ə)nt/	n.	瞬间,片刻
extra	/'ɛkstrə/	adj.	额外的,补充的,附加的
coupon	/'ku:pɒn/	n.	优惠券
expect	/ɪk'spɛkt, ɛk-/	v.	期望;预料

Phrases and Expressions

be able to	能够
pick up	拿起
deal with	应付；对待
bring in	赚（钱）

Note

recorded robot: 这里指电话录音。

Source: http://sbinfocanada.about.com/od/customerservice/a/custservrules.htm

Exercises

I. Summary

Directions: Fill in the blanks with the appropriate words according to your understanding.

Good customer service is the (1) _____ of any business. Good customer service is all about (2) _____ the customers back. Make sure that someone is (3) _____ the phone when someone calls your business, and don't make promises unless you will (4) _____ them. If you give the (5) _____ your attention, you may be able to please this one person this one time. And let your customer talk and show him that you are listening by making the appropriate (6) _____. Try your best to help the customers even if you can not get (7)_____ at that time. What's more, you should also train your staff to be always (8) _____ , (9) _____ and (10) _____.

II. Reading Comprehension

Directions: Fill in the blanks of the following two statements according to the text.

1. You give every member of your staff enough information and power to make those _____ decisions.

2. If you can get some of those customers to come back, your business will be _____ for long.

III. Vocabulary & Structures

Directions: Fill in the blanks with the proper expressions in the box.

| promotion | feedback | pick up | frustrate | extra |
| profitable | consistently | make a promise | deal with | discount |

1. His _____ means a raise in salary.
2. I hope you have found this article helpful and I welcome any _____.
3. _____ the receiver and drop a coin into the slot.
4. I know I _____ you sometimes, but I'll change.
5. What should they do with this _____ income?
6. You should give us _____ for such large quantity.
7. She makes a _____ for him.
8. Don't _____ when you are not sure you can do it.
9. This is a policy we have pursued _____.
10. A project should be _____ in every sense, if at all possible.

IV. Translation

Directions: Put the following English sentences into Chinese.

1. In the fall, I tell myself, I will start work and find an apartment and then I'll be a genuine adult.
2. We can deliver what you need to your office.
3. Step back and you will find a good way to solve the problem.
4. The house has a garage attached to it.
5. People like to be around positive people, not energy vampires.

Part III Strategies

写作解析

　　写作题主要考察应用文写作,包括感谢信、道歉信、邀请信、投诉信以及能填写表格,包括电话留言、简历和电子邮件等。这部分分值占总分的15%,作文字数要求不少于80个英语单词。首先要迅速审题,明确自己要表达的内容和写作目的,然后根据题目要求,选择正确的语言形式和风格来表达思想,写完之后,要通读全文,对拼写、语法等方面进行修改,注意保持书写的工整和卷面的整洁。要想拿高分,平时应多模仿范文,掌握应用文写作格式。下面以电子邮件为例说明写作部分解题技巧。

　　电子邮件,也就是我们常说的E-MAIL,随着计算机及互联网的广泛应用,电子邮件已经成为人们日常生活必要的联系方式。它和传统信件相同,均需要填入电子邮箱地址、主题词、正文和尾部落款部分。

【例】2005年12月实考题

说明：根据下列内容写一分电子邮件

发件人：JOHN SMITH（js456@vip.163.com）

收件人：假日酒店（电子油箱 marketing @ expedia.com）

发件时间：12月10号

事由：

1. 因行程改变，取消12月5号以JOHN SMITH的名义在贵酒店预订的12月12号到15号的两个单人房间。
2. 表示歉意，并询问是否需支付违约金。
3. 要求回信确认。

Words for reference：

违约金 cancellation penalty；假日酒店 Holiday Inn；以……的名义 in the name of；确认 confirm

参考范文：

To: Holiday Inn (marketing @ expedia.com)

From: JOHN SMITH（js456@vip.163.com）

Date: Dec.10

Subject: Reservation cancellation

Dear Sir or Madam,

  I am very sorry to inform you owing to the schedule change of our journey we have to cancel our reservation for the two single rooms from Dec.12 to 15 at your hotel under the name of John Smith reserved on Dec 5, 2005. Would you please write us back to confirm the cancellation? And also notify us if there is a cancellation penalty. Thanks very much.

Yours faithfully,
John Smith

【例】2007年6月实考题

说明：假定你是王军。根据以下内容以第一人称发一封电子邮件。

内容：

1. 发件人：王军
2. 收件人：Anna
3. 发件人电子邮件地址：wangjunll007@hotmail.corn
4. 收件人电子邮件地址：annall008@hotmail.com
5. 事由：

  王军在网站www.ebay.com.cn上卖出了一本书，书名《电子商务导论》。买家是美国客户Anna Brown。

6. 邮件涉及内容：

　　1）感谢对方购买《电子商务导论》；

　　2）书已寄出，预计一周内到达；

　　3）希望收到书后在网站上留下反馈意见；

　　4）如果满意，希望向其他客户推荐；

　　5）最近还会推出一些新的书，欢迎选购，再次购买可以享受折扣。

Words for reference：

反馈意见 feedback；电子商务导论 Introduction to E-commerce

注意：e-mail 的内容要写成一个段落，不得逐条罗列。

参考范文：

To: Anna Brown (annall008@hotmail.com)

From: Wang Jun（wangjunll007@hotmail,corn）

Subject: Feedback of the transaction

Dear Miss Anna Brown,

　　Thank you very much for buying the book of Introduction to E-commerce on the website of www.ebay.com.cn. I have mailed the book and it is due to arrive in a week. I hope you will give your feedback on the website after receiving the book. If you are satisfied with the book, please recommend it to other customers. Soon we are going to put out more new books online and you are more than welcome to check them out. When you make a purchase from us for the second time, you will enjoy a special discount. Thanks again for your business.

Yours faithfully,
Wang Jun

练习：假设你买了冰箱，但是冰箱有问题，请写一封投诉信来说明问题并提出要求解决问题的条件。

Part IV Applied Writing

Complaint Letter (投诉信)

投诉信是日常生活和日常交往中常见的英文信题材，是对产品或服务表示不满的信件，一般分三个部分：1. 提出投诉内容；2. 说明具体情况；3. 提出解决办法。

投诉信应重点表明投诉的原因，叙事应客观、准确、简洁。最后提出的解决方法应切实可行。在表达自己的不满时，语言要把握分寸，不失风度。

Sample 1:

Dear Sir,

　　I am happy that the refrigerator we ordered last week has arrived on time. But it is a great pity that we find there is something wrong with the refrigerator.

　　After we used it for several days, we found that food stored in the refrigerating compartment quickly turned bad. When we finally decided to take the temperature in it, we were surprised to find it was around 15℃, far from the standard temperature.

　　Would you please send a repairman to check on it as soon as possible? I hope that my problem will get your kind consideration.

Yours faithfully,
Li Ming

Sample 2:

Dear Mr. Chang,

　　On September 10, our order for 280 men's cotton sweaters was duly received, but we regret to say that 40 of them in white color were seriously soiled.

　　We investigated this issue immediately, and the result shows the damage was due to improper packing, for which the suppliers are definitely responsible.

　　Needless to say, we have suffered a great loss from this, as we cannot sell the sweaters in this condition to our customers. We ask you to conduct an investigation at your end and reply to us as soon as possible.

Sincerely yours,
Li Ming

Expressions for Making a Complaint

> complain against sb. about something ……投诉……
> I am writing to you to complain about ……我写信是为了投诉……
> I am writing to express my dissatisfaction with ……我写信是为了对……表示不满……
> Please let me know your solution to this matter.
> 请告知我你将如何处理这件事。
> I look forward to receiving a replacement as soon as possible.
> 我期待着尽快收到调换品。

Assignment: *Suppose you bought a washing machine and later found a worrisome problem. Write a letter of complaint to describe the problem and request a solution.*

Part V Cultural Express

Wal-Mart Business Culture

Open Door

Our management believes open communication is critical to understanding and meeting our associates' and our customers' needs. Associates can trust and rely on the open door policy; it's one of the most important parts of our culture.

Sundown Rule

Observing the Sundown Rule means we do our best to answer requests by the close of business on the day we receive them. Whether it's a request from a store across the country or a call from down the hall, we do our very best to give each other and our customers same-day service. We do this by combining our efforts and depending upon each other to get things done.

Grass Roots Process

Sam's philosophy lives on today in Walmart's Grass Roots Process, our formal way of capturing associates' ideas, suggestions and concerns.

3 Basic Beliefs & Values

Our unique culture has helped make Walmart one of the world's most admired companies. Since Sam Walton opened Walmart in 1962, our culture has rested on three basic beliefs. We live out these beliefs each day in our interactions with our customers and each other.

10-Foot Rule

The 10-foot Rule is one of our secrets to customer service. During his many store visits, Sam Walton encouraged associates (employees) to take this pledge with him: "I promise that whenever I come within 10 feet of a customer, I will look him in the eye, greet him, and ask if I can help him."

Servant Leadership

Sam Walton believed that effective leaders do not lead from behind their desks. "It's more important than ever that we develop leaders who are servants, who listen to their partners—their associates—in a way that creates wonderful morale to help the whole team accomplish an overall goal," Sam said.

Teamwork

Sam Walton, our founder, believed in the power of teamwork. As our stores grow and the pace of modern life quickens, that philosophy of teamwork has only become more important over the years.

Walmart Cheer

Don't be surprised if you hear our associates shouting this enthusiastically at your local Walmart store. It's our cheer, and while it might not sound serious, we take it seriously. It's one way we show pride in our company.

Associate Stories

Read inspiring stories from associates (employees) that carry out our beliefs and values every day.

拓展词汇

A friendship founded on business is better than business founded on friendship. (John Davision Rockefeller, American businessman)
建立在商务基础上的友谊胜过建立在友谊基础上的商务。(美国实业家 洛克菲勒 J.D.)

Advertising may be described as the science of arresting human intelligence long enough to get money from it. (Leacock Stephen, Canadian economist)
广告可被视为一种长久蒙蔽人类智慧以期从中赚钱的技巧。(加拿大经济学家 斯蒂芬 L.)

All progress is based upon a universal innate desire on the part of every organism to live beyond its income. (Samuel Butler, British writer)
世人莫不怀着一种与生俱来的欲望,要把支出超过收入,此乃一切进步的动力。(英国作家 勃特勒 S.)

Avarice , the spur of industry. (David Hume, British Philosopher)
贪婪是工业的兴奋剂。(英国哲学家 休谟 D.)

Did you ever expect a corporation to have a conscience, when it has no soul to be damned, and no body to be kicked? (Edward Thurlow, British Lawyer)
公司既没有灵魂可以被诅咒,又没有躯体可以被踢翻,难道你指望它有什么良心吗?(英国律师 瑟洛杉矶 E.)

For years I thought what was good for our country was good for General Motors, and vice versa. (Charles E. Wilison American president of GM)
多少年来,我始终认为对国家有利的事对我们通用汽车公司也有利,反之亦然。(美国通用汽车公司总裁 威尔逊 C.E.)

Good times, bad times, there will always be advertising. In good times people want advertising; in bad times they have to have it. (Bruce Barton British economist)
不管是繁荣时期还是萧条时期,广告总会存在。繁荣时,人们想做广告;萧条时,人们不得不做广告。(英国经济学家 巴顿 B.)

The trouble with the profit system has always been that is highly unprofitable to most people. (E.B.White, American writer)
利润制度的最大弊端始终是绝大多数的人是绝对无利可图的。(美国作家 怀特 E.B.)

There can be no economy where there is no efficiency. (Disraeli, British statesman)
没有效率就没有经济。(英国政治家 狄斯雷利)

There is no resting place for an enterprise in a competitive economy. (Alfred P. Sloan, American businessman)
在竞争的经济中,没有企业休息的地方。(美国实业家 斯隆 A.D.)

Unit 5

Culture Shock

Learning Objectives:

You are able to:
- ☞ Learn to recommend scenic spots to foreigners
- ☞ Fulfill a Reservation Form
- ☞ Arrange tourings to some scenic spots
- ☞ Comment on scenic spots
- ☞ Write a welcome speech/letter

You are suggested to:
- ☞ Recognize the English expressions of some scenic spots
- ☞ Be familiar with some traditional Chinese Craftwork

• Unit 5   Culture Shock •

Part I   Listening and Speaking

Warm-up

Task 1

Directions: Do you know their Chinese version? Try to say something about some of them.

chopsticks	Tangzhuang	Zongzi	folding fans
Chinese Fancy Knots	Taiji	Dragon Boats	Beijing Hutong
Chinese Kongfu	cloisonné vase	Yinyang Sign	

Task 2

Directions: Work with your partner and match the Chinese with its English equivalent.

边界乐园 ☆   ★ Main Street
主街 ☆   ★ Adventureland
新奥尔良广场 ☆   ★ New Orleans Square
冒险乐园 ☆   ★ Frontierland
幻想世界 ☆   ★ Critter Country
未来世界 ☆   ★ Fantasyland
动物王国 ☆   ★ Mickey's Toontown
米奇卡通城 ☆   ★ Tomorrowland

Oral Practice

Task 1

Directions: Read the dialogue and answer the following questions.

W: I've heard that those who have been to China buy cloisonné vases as souvenirs. I'd also like to buy some.

M: Our shop is the biggest dealer in the city. Every day we get hundreds of tourists coming in to buy different sizes of cloisonné vases. Please feel free to select from any of them.

W: I'd like a pair of medium-sized cloisonné vases with a light blue background.

M: How do you like this one? The background is pale blue with traditional Chinese paintings of flowers and birds.

W: It's gorgeous. How much is it?

M: One hundred and fifty yuan.

W: Can you come down on the price a little bit?

M: I'm very sorry, madam, but our shop holds a one-price policy. We are not allowed to change the price at will.

W: I see. I'll take a pair then. I am sure my husband will like them.

M: I'm sure he will.

W: Can you pack the vases and send them to the United States for me?

M: Yes, we can. The postage will be an extra charge of one hundred and thirty-eight yuan. There is another extra charge of fifteen yuan for the packing, because we will have to pack them in a special box so that they won't get broken.

W: All right. Here's the money.

M: Can you write down your name and mailing address on this slip?

W: Sure.

• Unit 5　Culture Shock •

1. What would A like to buy as souvenirs?
   ☐ Medium-sized cloisonné vases.　　☐ Chinese paintings .
2. Where does the dialogue take place?
   ☐ Bookstore.　　☐ Souvenir shop.
3. How much does one vase cost?
   ☐ One hundred and fifty yuan.
   ☐ One hundred and fifteen yuan.

Task 2

Directions: Suppose you are going to visit HongKong Disneyland. Here is the Park Hours and Calendar for you to read. Role-play a conversation with your partner to discuss your tour schedule. Then reverse the roles and do it again.

Daily Calendar

　　See **park hours**, **fireworks** and **show times**! These times are provided for your reference and may change on the day of your visit. On the day of your visit, please **collect the Times Guide** at Guest Relations for more information about that day's shows, including any revisions to the schedule.

June 5, 2012 (Tuesday)
Park Hours 乐园时间
This is a Standard Day. 10:30AM - 8:00PM
Parade and Firework Times 巡游及烟花表演时间
Flights of Fantasy Parade 迪士尼飞天巡游
Begins in Fantasyland, near the entrance of Storybook Theatre　3:30PM
'Disney in the Stars' Fireworks「星梦奇缘」烟花表演
This spectacular fireworks show transforms the sky above Sleeping Beauty Castle into a stunning evening spectacle 8:00 PM

Special Hours: 个别开放时间
Toy Story Land 反斗奇兵大本营 11:00AM — 5:45PM
Toy Story Land attractions will close approximately 1.5 hours before the fireworks spectacular. Depending on the day's attendance, the closing time of the attractions may be earlier.
Main Street, U.S.A. 美国小镇大街
Animation Academy(动画艺术教室) (Show performs in Cantonese) (以广东话演出) 10:40AM — 7:40PM
Stage Shows 剧场演出
Adventureland 探险世界
'**Festival of the Lion King**'「狮子王庆典」
If you would like to watch the show with Simplified Chinese subtitles, please be seated at the last 6 rows. 12:00PM; 2:00PM; 4:30PM; 6:00PM
Fantasyland 幻想世界
'**The Golden Mickeys**'「米奇金奖音乐剧」12:45PM; 1:45PM; 4:00PM; 5:00PM; 6:15PM
'**Stitch Encounter**'「幸会史迪仔」
Please check for show times in your preferred language (in Cantonese / in Putonghua or in English) at the attraction entrance.
Character Greeting Times 与迪士尼朋友见面
Characters appear occasionally at the following locations, see map for locations:
Main Street, U.S.A 美国小镇大街
Town Square 小镇广场 10:30AM — 4:45PM
Fantasyland 幻想世界
Fantasy Gardens 梦想花园 12:00PM — 6:30PM
Sleeping Beauty Castle 睡公主城堡 10:30AM — 5:30PM
Tomorrowland 明日世界 11:00AM — 5:15PM

• Unit 5   Culture Shock •

Listening Practice

Task 1

Directions: Listen to the dialogues and tick (√) in the box at the end of the correct answer.

1. Where does the tourist come from?
    A. Suzhou. ☐
    B. the Gusu Travel Agency. ☐
    C. America. ☐
2. Where is the tourist visiting in China?
    A. Suzhou. ☐
    B. China. ☐
    C. America. ☐
3. What is the other name of Suzhou?
    A. beautiful city. ☐
    B. the Venice of the East. ☐
    C. the Oriental Pearl. ☐
4. How many gardens are there in Suzhou?
    A. 150 gardens. ☐
    B. 115 gardens. ☐
    C. 50 gardens. ☐
5. How long will the tourist tour in Suzhou?
    A. one day. ☐
    B. three days. ☐
    C. a week. ☐

Task 2

Directions: In this section you will hear a recorded short passage. The passage will be read three times. You are required to put the missing words or phrases in the numbered blanks according to what you hear.

　　Styles of (1) _____ , including initial conversations and nonverbal rituals, vary among individuals and(2) _____ . The introduction of a university president to a new professor is considerably (3) _____ than that of two people of the same status in the social situation. At a(4) _____ , an introduction is likely to be more formal than one made at a party. (5) _____ , styles of introductions vary from country to country. Bowing to (6) _____ is customary in parts of the Far East. In the (7) _____ Hemisphere and in other parts of the world, (8) _____ is the common practice. Putting the palm of the hand to(9) _____ is traditional in North Africa. Despite the cultural variations, the purpose of all introductions is always the same—to provide an (10) _____ for people to get to know each other.

Task 3

Directions: Listen to the conversation and work in pairs to fill in the form given below.

Reservation Form:

Name of Guest: Mr./Mrs./Miss/Ms _____
Telephone number: _____
Places to visit: _____
Days for touring: _____
Number of tourists: _____
Date: _____
Price: _____

Part II Reading

Text A

Before Reading:

1. Are you familiar with the following pictures? Have you ever been there? How do you feel about them?

2. Talk with your partner about the differences between Chinese theme parks (主题公园) and Disneyland.

Chinese theme parks	Disneyland

Disney Culture Shock

Before Hong Kong Disneyland opened last year, planners were careful to build the park according to the rules of fengshui. They made sure to serve Chinese food; they also built a garden of costumed characters, since the Chinese like taking photos. However, a free event that was held before the official opening was noisy and overcrowded. Mainland Chinese tourists visiting Hong Kong Disneyland on that day smoked in non-smoking areas, went barefoot and even let children urinate in public. The Apple Daily described the behavior of mainland tourists as "disgraceful" while acknowledging that they "brought good business" to the park as it opened its gates on Monday to 16,000 visitors. Meanwhile, local famous stars were offended by rude treatment. Health officials were stopped from entering the park in uniform. Environmentalists protested the shark-fin soup on the menus. This experience raised questions about Disneyland's ability to operate well in this culture. It also raised concerns about what will happen when the company opens its first park on the mainland, in Shanghai, in a few years.

"If they got into trouble in Hong Kong, it is certain they will get into trouble on the mainland." said Chan Kin Man, a professor at the Chinese University of Hong Kong. "Disneyland is a symbol of the West. When relations between the United States and China turn sour, it might turn into a target," Chan said.

Despite several sold-out days over Christmas, Disney was unprepared for the early reaction to a promotion during the Lunar New Year. Hundreds of already ticketed customers were locked out because the park was full. Everything was in disorder: crying children, angry parents and tourists climbing fences to get in.

Disney called the problems "growing pains". They found it difficult to move forward since they had a group of people who were fond of anything Western, but they also had a strong group of nationalists. In order to offer a more satisfying service, Hong Kong Disneyland has made changes, and then there were signs of some success.

Huang Xianyi, 50, a bank clerk from mainland China, was among the first to arrive at Hong Kong Disneyland on a recent Sunday. By midmorning, he was waiting in line, watching the shows of "The Hunchback of Notre Dame", "Mulan", "The Little Mermaid" and "Woodpecker", etc.

"I liked the rhythm of the show.

Themes ranged from adventure to romance, the adventure stories were exciting and comfortable to watch. It suits both children and adults," Huang said. "All those stories remind me of my childhood." "I don't expect to see many Chinese things in Disneyland."

"They do need to improve communications with the public and make sure that they connect with the local people," added John Ap, a theme park expert.

"Understanding the Chinese market takes time," Ap said. "They can learn a lot from the case in Hong Kong Disneyland. I am certain that they'll be a lot more careful when they go into the mainland China."

New Words

（标★为A级词汇，标☆为超纲词汇）

overcrowded	/ˌəʊvəˈkraʊdɪd/	adj.	过度拥挤的
barefoot	/ˈbɛəfʊt/	adj.	赤脚的
☆urinate	/ˈjʊərɪneɪt/	v.	小便
disgraceful	/dɪsˈgreɪsfʊl, -f(ə)l/	adj.	可耻的
★acknowledge	/əkˈnɒlɪdʒ/	v.	承认（事实、局面等）
offend	/əˈfɛnd/	v.	冒犯
uniform	/ˈjuːnɪfɔːm/	n.	制服
environmentalist	/ɪnˌvaɪrənˈmɛnt(ə)lɪst, ɛn-/	n.	环保人士
★protest	/protest/	v.	抗议
reaction	/rɪˈakʃ(ə)n/	n.	反应
disorder	/dɪsˈɔːdə/	n.	混乱
nationalist	/ˈnaʃ(ə)n(ə)lɪst/	n.	民族主义者
rhythm	/ˈrɪð(ə)m/	n.	节奏
★adventure	/ədˈvɛntʃə/	n.	冒险
romance	/rə(ʊ)ˈmans, ˈrəʊmans/	n.	浪漫史
communication	/kəmjuːnɪˈkeɪʃ(ə)n/	n.	通讯

Phrases and Expressions

turn sour		变得让人扫兴
growing pains		发展时期（尤指初期）的困难
The Hunchback of Notre Dame		钟楼驼侠
Mulan		花木兰
The Little Mermaid	/ˈmɜːmeɪd/	小美人鱼
Woodpecker	/ˈwʊdpɛkə/	啄木鸟

● Unit 5 Culture Shock ●

Exercises

I. Reading Comprehension

Directions: Circle the right answer for the following questions.

1. According to what rules was Hong Kong Disneyland build?
   A. The park was built according to the rules of fengshui.
   B. The park was built according to the rules of Western architecture.
   C. The park was built according to the rules of Hong Kong architecture.
   D. The park was built according to the rules of American architecture.
2. What did The Apple Daily think of the behavior of mainland tourists? The paper described it as _____.
   A. overcrowded
   B. disgraceful
   C. rude
   D. successful
3. What questions were raised after Hong Kong Disneyland's first opening?
   A. What will happen when the company opens its first park on the mainland, in Shanghai, in a few years.
   B. Whether Disneyland has the ability to operate well in Chinese culture.
   C. When will Disneyland open in Shanghai.
   D. Whether Disneyland will open on mainland, China.
4. What happened in Disney's promotion during the Lunar New Year?
   A. Hundreds of already ticketed customers were locked out because the park was full.
   B. Everything was in disorder.
   C. There were crying children, angry parents and tourists climbing fences to get in.
   D. All of Above.
5. What does the "growing pains" of Disney refer to?
   A. They found it difficult to move forward.
   B. A group of people were fond of anything Western.
   C. There was a strong group of nationalists.
   D. How to suit both the needs of nationalists and Western-lovers.

II. Word Usage

Directions: Complete each of the following sentences with the correct form of the italicized word given in the brackets.

1. I am always _____ *(care)* when crossing a street.
2. He _____ *(official)* remains head of the government.
3. The place was _____ *(overcrowd)* with tourists.
4. Our city is _____ *(grow)* rapidly.
5. Unemployment pay is _____ *(disgraceful)* low.
6. There were too many things in the small _____ *(disorder)* room.
7. That love story is very _____ *(romance)*.
8. In the process of coal mining, people used to pay attention to the coal production only, and overlook _____ *(environment)* protection.
9. His _____ *(react)* was quite unexpected.
10. I yelled at him _____ *(angry)*.

III. Blank Filling

Directions: Translate the Chinese part of the following sentences with the correct form of the words and expressions in the box.

according to	go barefoot	get into trouble	turn sour
unprepared for	in disorder	be fond of	range from
make sure	in public		

1. The prices of these goods _____ several dollars to several hundred dollars. (不等)
2. We used to play together, live together, complete the education together, _____ together. (闯祸)
3. It's human nature for parents to _____ their children. (钟爱)
4. It's no pity to see a woman weep than a goose _____. (光脚)
5. She was totally _____ this incident. (毫无准备)
6. The meeting finished _____. (一片混乱)
7. File the letters _____ dates. (按照)
8. My hip hop skills will never _____. (不会变差)
9. I'll _____ she is ready for you. (确认)
10. I'm not used to speaking _____. (当众)

IV. Translation

Directions: Put the following English sentences into Chinese.

1. Before Hong Kong Disneyland opened last year, planners were careful to build the park according to the rules of Fengshui.
2. Environmentalists protested the shark-fin soup on the menus.
3. If they got into trouble in Hong Kong, it is certain they will get into trouble on the mainland.
4. Hundreds of already ticketed customers were locked out because the park was full.
5. Everything was in disorder: crying children, angry parents and tourists climbing fences to get in.

V. True or false

Directions: Decide whether the following statements are true or false according to the text. Write "T" if the statement is true and "F" if it is false.

_____ 1. They only serve Chinese food in Hong Kong Disneyland.
_____ 2. Tourists can smoke in non-smoking areas in Disney.
_____ 3. When the relations between the United States and China turn sour, Disney will turn into a bridge to connect two countries.
_____ 4. Disney's "growing pains" means that it is painful to grow bigger and bigger.
_____ 5. Disney needs to improve communications with the public.

Text B

Before Reading:

1. What is culture shock? Use your own words to describe it, and then give some examples.
2. Do you agree that awareness of cultural differences can bridge the gap of misunderstanding? Why or why not?

How to Handle Business Culture Shock

In our increasingly globalized world, more and more professionals find themselves traveling to new places and interacting with foreigners, as the companies they work for expand and develop new business relationships. When dealing with these interactions, whether they will be on brief business trips or visits, or extended stays, it is more important than ever to be aware of the cultural differences and sensitivities of all parties involved in the interaction. Minor cultural blunders that are easily overlooked in social interactions can become serious misbehaviors when applied to the work environment, where important business deals, respect and efficiency are at stake.

When embarking on a business relationship with members of another culture there are some fundamental points to take into consideration in order to avoid misunderstanding and endangering what could otherwise be a beneficial interaction for both groups.

Do your prospective partners come from a more individualistic or collectivistic society?

This is important because it can affect both the way the other company makes decisions, and the way they view you. Americans tend to be more individualistic and can be perceived as aggressive in their business dealings. Collectivistic societies tend to rely on input from a number of people. Some cultures, such as in most Hispanic societies, wish to get to know their prospective business partners on a more personal level before actually undertaking business with them. In these cultures it is often considered rude or untrustworthy to skip the small-talk and interact on a strictly professional level.

Is structure or flexibility more valued?

Learning how a culture perceives time and deadlines saves a lot of confusion and frustration for everyone. While some cultures are very strict about scheduling and structure, others perceive these to be less important than actually achieving the established objectives in a satisfactory and thorough manner. Sometimes it is not a "one-or-another" answer. For the Chinese, punctuality depends on the importance of the occasion and the people they are going to meet.

What kind of communication style is appreciated?

While in some cultures, strongly expressing emotions during business dealings is acceptable; in others, such as with the Japanese, this is considered inappropriate. It is useful to find out what kinds of emotional expression are considered negative by the other culture, in order to avoid unwittingly making a bad impression.

How much formality is appreciated?

It is also important to know how formally people interact in a working environment. To some cultures, relative informality and familiarity among workmates or superiors is acceptable; for others, it is a shocking sign of disrespect and a breach of personal space. While Latin-based cultures are generally noted for their warm behavior, they generally strictly adhere to rules of social propriety as is seen by the common use of the third person when addressing superiors or elders. That is also the case in many Asian cultures such as China, Japan and Korea. The social manner and language make a difference at the cross culture workplace. Attempting to dissuade someone from this practice often results in feelings of discomfort and invasion of space, since familiar speech is frequently reserved for family members and close friends only.

In the cross-culture business relationship, people should keep an open mind and try not to form an opinion about the new culture too soon. In addition, developing cultural awareness will limit simple misunderstandings from becoming international business blunders.

New Words

（标★为A级词汇，标☆为超纲词汇）

☆globalize	/ˈgləʊb(ə)lʌɪz/	v.	（使）全球化
★professional	/prəˈfeʃ(ə)n(ə)l/	n.	专业人士
extended	/ɪkˈstendɪd, ek-/	adj.	扩大的
sensitivity	/ˌsensɪˈtɪvɪti/	n.	敏感
blunder	/ˈblʌndə/	n.	疏忽
★overlook	/əʊvəˈlʊk/	v.	忽视
misbehavior	/ˌmɪsbɪˈheɪvjə(r)/	n.	不礼貌
endanger	/ɪnˈdeɪn(d)ʒə, en-/	v.	使遭受危险
☆prospective	/prəˈspektɪv/	adj.	预期的
individualistic	/ˌɪndɪvɪdjʊəˈlɪstɪk/	adj.	个人主义的
★collectivistic	/kəˈlektɪvɪztɪk/	adj.	集体主义的
perceive	/pəˈsiːv/	v.	注意到
aggressive	/əˈgresɪv/	adj.	侵略的
undertake	/ʌndəˈteɪk/	v.	承担
untrustworthy	/ʌnˈtrʌs(t)wəːði/	adj.	不能信赖的
skip	/skɪp/	v.	略过
☆flexibility	/ˌfleksɪˈbɪlɪti/	n.	柔韧性
deadline	/ˈdedlʌɪn/	n.	最后期限
confusion	/kənˈfjuːʒ(ə)n/	n.	混乱
★frustration	/frʌˈstreɪʃn/	n.	失败
schedule	/ˈʃedjuːl, ˈsked-/	v.	安排
objective	/əbˈdʒektɪv/	adj.	客观的
thorough	/ˈθʌrə/	adj.	彻底的
★punctuality	/ˌpʌŋ(k)tʃʊˈalɪti/	n.	严守时间
inappropriate	/ɪnəˈprəʊprɪət/	adj.	不恰当的
negative	/ˈnegətɪv/	adj.	消极的
unwittingly	/ʌnˈwɪtɪŋli/	adv.	不知情地

formality	/fɔːˈmælɪti/	n.	礼节
familiarity	/fəmɪlɪˈærɪti/	n.	通晓
superior	/suːˈpɪərɪə, sjuː-/	n.	上级
☆breach	/briːtʃ/	v.	违背
dissuade	/dɪˈsweɪd/	v.	劝阻
invasion	/ɪnˈveɪʒ(ə)n/	n.	侵犯
★reserved	/rɪˈzɜːvd/	adj.	矜持的
awareness	/əˈwɛːnəs/	n.	意识

Phrases and Expressions

culture shock		文化冲击
interact with	/ɪntərˈækt/	与……相互影响
at stake	/steɪk/	濒于险境
embark on	/ɪmˈbɑːk, em-/	着手
take into consideration	/kənsɪdəˈreɪʃ(ə)n/	考虑到
adhere to	/ədˈhɪə/	坚持
social propriety		社会习俗

Exercises

I. Summary

Directions: Fill in the blanks with the appropriate words according to your understanding.

In the increasingly (1) _____ world, more and more professionals travel to new places and interact with foreign people. The key to avoid (2) _____ in the cross-culture business is to keep an open mind, try not to form an opinion about the new culture too soon, and develop the (3) _____. You should get to know the following four questions. First, try to judge whether your prospective partners come from a more (4) _____ or (5) _____ society. This is important because it can affect both the way the other company makes decisions, and the way they view you. Second, is structure or (6) _____ more valued? Because learning how a culture perceives time and deadlines saves a lot of (7) _____ and frustration for everyone. Third, what kind of (8) _____ is appreciated? It is useful to find out what kinds of (9) _____ are considered negative by the other culture, in order to avoid unwittingly making a bad impression. Finally, it is also important to know how (10) _____ people interact in a working environment.

II. Reading Comprehension

Directions: Fill in the blanks of the following two statements according to the text..

1. In cross-cultural communications, it is more important than ever to be aware of the cultural _____ and _____ of all parties involved in the interaction.
2. To some cultures, relative _____ and _____ among workmates or superiors is acceptable; for others, it is a shocking sign of disrespect and a breach of personal space.

III. Vocabulary & Structures

Directions: Fill in the blanks with the proper expressions in the box.

| at stake | embark on | adhere to | interact with | deal with |
| be aware of | be involved in | apply to | be noted for | in order to |

1. This nation _____ its economic stability.
2. His reputation was _____.
3. School regulations _____ every student.
4. We must _____ the open policy.
5. I have some business to _____.
6. However, we all need to _____ the potential risks.
7. When we _____ any task, it is important that we start well.
8. Teachers have a limited amount of time to _____ each child.
9. She didn't want to _____ trouble.
10. We breathe _____ live.

IV. Translation

Directions: Put the following English sentences into Chinese.

1. When dealing with these interactions, whether they will be on brief business trips or visits, or extended stays, it is more important than ever to be aware of the cultural differences and sensitivities of all parties involved in the interaction.
2. Americans tend to be more individualistic and can be perceived as aggressive in their business dealings.
3. For the Chinese, punctuality depends on the importance of the occasion and the people they are going to meet.
4. It is also important to know how formally people interact in a working environment.
5. In the cross-culture business, keep an open mind, try not to form an opinion about the new culture too soon, and develop cultural awareness.

Part III Strategies

阅读解析（一）

在B级阅读理解考试中，Task 1 和 Task 2 的题型相同，分别有一小段短文，每段后有5道阅读理解题，每道题后附4个备选答案。在真题试卷中，阅读理解中 Task 1 和 Task 2 后的题目序号是从36至45排列。

一、识别细节题

在PRETCO(B)阅读理解题 Task 1 和 Task 2 中，识别细节题比较多。做这类题目首先应先将题目浏览一遍，再带着问题看文章，在文章相关内容中寻找所需信息。基本上所有问题的答案都能在文章中的相应段落某些句子中直接找到答案。（因为篇幅问题，以下所选的例题中凡是和答题无关的段落和句子基本上全部略去，答案出处的句子皆以下划线标出。）

【例】2009年12月实考题
Task 1:
第一自然段中的句子：
　　Thank you for your interest in Calibre Cassette (盒式录音带) library. This letter tells you about our service. With it we are sending you an application form, so that you can join if you would like to try it.
　　Calibre library aims to provide the pleasure of reading to anyone who cannot read ordinary print books because of sight problems. We currently have over 7,000 books available for reading for pleasure, including 1,000 especially for children. All our books are recorded cover-to-cover on ordinary cassettes and can be played on any cassette player. They are sent and returned by post, free of charge....

36. According to the first paragraph, the library sends the application form to the readers so that they can _____.

　　A. read ordinary books　　　　B. order cassette players
　　C. buy Calibre cassette　　　　D. use the library service

　　从该段最后两句话中可以看出，图书馆寄送申请表给读者的目的是让他们加入图书馆并享受其服务。因此该题应选 D。

38. The service of sending and returning books by post is _____.
   A. not available to children   B. paid by the users
   C. free of charge   D. not provided

根据内容和句子可以判断出该题答案应为C。

二、主旨大意题

主旨大意题主要考察学生对整篇文章或某一段落大意的理解，要求考生能确定文章的主题(main point)、中心思想(main idea)或给文章拟一个合适的标题(title)。英语短文的主题或中心思想通常在文章的第一句或每小段的第一句表现出来，但也有在文章中间或在文章最后出现的，因此做这种题目常可在这些地方找到与答案有关的信息。

主旨大意题常用的提问句式：
(1) The passage is mainly about _____.
(2) A proper title for this passage would be _____.

【例】2009年12月实考题
Task 1:
第一自然段中的句子:
　　Thank you for your interest in Calibre Cassette (盒式录音带) library. This letter tells you about our service...

40. The main purpose of this letter is to _____.
   A. introduce the library's service to readers   B. recommend new books to the readers
   C. send a few catalogues to readers   D. express thanks to the readers

　　在第一自然段中，从第一句和第二句中，就可以直接找到答案，选出A项。

【例】2006年6月实考题
Task 1:
第一自然段中的句子：
Unlike Britain, the U.S. does not have a national health care service...
第二自然段中的句子：
In Britain, when people are ill, they usually go to a family doctor first.
...

40. Which of the following would be the best title for this passage?

    A. Types of Doctors in the United States

    B. Health care in the United States and Britain

    C. Treatment of Sick Children in the United States

    D. Medical Insurance in the United States and Britain

引句为 Task 1 的第一自然段第一句和第二段自然中的第一句。从第一段就可以看出 B 是正确答案,而第二段第一句更进一步予以证实。

三、逻辑推理题

逻辑推理题要求考生根据作者的论述,做出一个合乎逻辑的结论。逻辑推理必须建立在文章所提供的事实基础上。考生首先应根据所提问题在文中寻找有关事实,再根据所提供的事实下结论。

必须注意的是:
考生不可根据自己的主观臆断,毫无依据地下结论。
所得结论应符合原文作者的意图。

逻辑推理题常用的提问句式:
From this passage, we can learn that _____.
According to the passage... is important because _____.
To ensure that ... you must _____.
In order to... one should _____.

【例】2009年12月实考题
Task 2:
第一自然段中的句子:
    People in some countries cannot use their native language for Web addresses. Neither can Chinese speakers, who have to rely on pinyin. But last Friday, ICANN, the Web's governing body, approved the use of up to 16 languages for the new system.

42. The approval of the use of 16 languages by ICANN will allow web users to _____.

    A. change their e-mail address

    B. E-mail their messages in characters

    C. have the chance to learn other languages

    D. use addresses in their own language

由引文可判断出，网络主管团体ICANN为新系统正式批准了最多16种语言的使用，而联系前两句话可以推知，此后网络使用者便可以在网址方面使用他们自己的语言了。因此本题应选D。

第二自然段中的句子：

...The change will also allow the suffix (后缀) to be expressed in 16 other alphabets, including traditional and simplified Chinese characters.

43. The new system will allow the suffix of a Web address to be expressed by_____.
    A. any native language   B. figures and numbers
    C. Chinese characters   D. symbols and signs

本题可使用逻辑推理法，由引文可知，四个选项中除了C，其他三项文中均未提到，故正确选项为C。

四、判断正误题

做判断题通常使用排除法，即从所提供的四个选项中逐一排除错误选项，剩下的便是正确的；反之，逐一排除正确的，剩下的便是错误的。

判断题常见的提问方式有：

Which of the following statements is TRUE?

According to the passage, which of the following statements is TRUE?

Which statement is NOT TRUE according to the passage?

【例】2007年12月实考题
Task 1:
第四自然段中的句子：

　　Volvo, a famous Swedish carmaker, was the first to use seat belts in 1949. Air bags are also very important for car safety, because sometimes a seat belt isn't enough. If the car is going really fast and runs into something, seat belts could even hurt the people who wear them.

38. Which of the following statements is TRUE?
    A. People with seat belts fastened will be always safe in cars.
    B. Volvo was the first carmaker to use seat belts in cars.
    C. Air bags will come out before the car hits something.
    D. All cars have air bags in front of the seats.

由引文可判断出,四个选项中B项是正确答案。

五、判断词义题

这种题目通常要求考生理解一个比较熟悉的词在新语境中的新内涵或者是解释一个不太熟悉的单词或短语。解答这样的题目需要抓住两个线索:词性线索和上下文线索。所谓抓住词性线索就是根据构词法判断词意;所谓上下文线索就是根据单词或短语前后的句子或段落来判断其意思。

判断词义题常用提问方式:
The word ... refers to _____.
The word ... means _____.
The phrase .... Means _____.

【例】2005年1月实考题
Task 1:
最后一段:

Jobs that are suited to telecommuting include writing, design work, computer programming and accounting. If a job involves working with information, a telecommuter can probably do it.

39. The phrase "suited to"(Line 1, Para 3) means _____.
  A. acceptable for B. difficult for C. fit for D. bad for

根据《基本要求》,suit 属于无标记词,即属于在中学阶段就应该掌握的1,000个常用词。它的意思是"适合,恰当"。suited是其过去分词,这里做形容词用,基本意思是"适合的,合适的"。由此我们可以判断suited to的意思就是fit for,故C项为正确答案。

【例】2007年6月实考题
Task 2:
第二自然段中的句子:

This decision was suitable for Los Angeles. The city grew outward instead of upward. Los Angeles never built many tall apartment buildings. Instead, people live in houses with gardens.

42. "The city grew outward instead of upward" means _____.
  A. the city became more spread out instead of growing taller
  B. there were few small houses than tall buildings
  C. rapid development in the city center
  D. many tall buildings could be found in the city

由引文可判断出,四个选项中A项是正确答案。

Practice

Directions: This part is to test your reading ability. There are 2 tasks for you to fulfill. After reading the following passages, you will find 5 questions. For each question or statement there are 4 choices marked A, B, C and D. You should make the correct choice.

Task 1

Online advertising is the means of selling a product on the Internet. With the arrival of the Internet, the business world has become digitalized(数字化)and people prefer buying things online, which is easier and faster. Online advertising is also known as e-advertising. It offers a great variety of services, which can not be offered by any other way of advertising.

One major benefit of online advertising is the immediate spread of information that is not limited by geography or time. Online advertising can be viewed day and night throughout the world. Besides, it reduces the cost and increases the profit of the company.

Small businesses especially find online advertising cheap and effective. They can focus on their ideal customers and pay very little for the advertisements.

In a word, online advertising is a cheap and effective way of advertising, whose success has so far fully proved its great potential (潜力).

1. According to the first paragraph, buying things online is more _____.
   A. convenient   B. fashionable   C. traditional   D. reliable
2. Compared with any other way of advertising, online advertising _____.
   A. attracts more customers   B. displays more samples
   C. offers more services   D. makes more profits
3. Which of the following statements is TRUE of online advertising?
   A. It has taken the place of traditional advertising.
   B. It will make the Internet technology more efficient.
   C. It can help sell the latest models of digitalized products.
   D. It can spread information without being limited by time.
4. Who can especially benefit from online advertising?
   A. Local companies.   B. Small businesses.
   C. Government departments   D. International organizations.
5. This passage is mainly about _____.
   A. the function and the use of the Internet   B. the application of digital technology
   C. the development of small businesses   D. the advantages of online advertising

105

Task 2

During our more than 60-year history, with our vast knowledge and experience, Trafalgar has created perfectly designed travel experiences and memories.

Exceptional value

Traveling with Trafalgar can save you up to 40% when compared with traveling independently. We can find you the right hotels, restaurants, and our charges include entrance fees, tolls (道路通行费) etc. Because we're the largest touring company with great buying power, we can pass on our savings to you.

Fast-track entrance

Traveling with us means no standing in line (排队) at major sights. Trafalgar takes care of all the little details, which means you are always at the front of the line.

Travel with like-minded friends

Because we truly are global, you will travel with English-speaking people from around the world, and that leads to life-long friendships.

Great savings

We provide many great ways to save money, including Early Payment Discount(折扣), Frequent Traveler Savings and more.

Fast check-in

Once your booking has been made, you are advised to check in online at our website and meet your fellow travelers before you leave.

6. Because of its great buying power, Trafalgar _____.
   A. can find the cheapest restaurants   B. can pass on its savings to tourists
   C. takes tourists to anywhere in the world   D. allows tourists to travel independently
7. Traveling with Trafalgar, tourists do not have to _____.
   A. bring their passports with them   B. pay for their hotels and meals
   C. stand in line at major sights   D. take their luggage with them
8. Traveling with Trafalgar, tourists may _____.
   A. meet tour guides from different countries
   B. make new friends from around the world
   C. win a special prize offered by the company
   D. have a good chance to learn foreign languages
9. Which of the following is mentioned as a way to earn a discount?
   A. Early payment.   B. Group payment.   C. Office booking.   D. Online booking.
10. After having made the booking, tourists are advised to check in _____.
    A. at the hotels   B. at the airport   C. by telephone   D. on the website

Part IV　Applied Writing

Welcome Speech/Letter (欢迎词)

　　常见的欢迎词分为两大类：一类用于现场口头发表的欢迎词，非正式表达；另一类用于书面表达的欢迎词，正式表达更为郑重。

　　欢迎词的书面表达特点具有欢愉性，用语简单且具有激情。常常是机关、企事业单位、社会团体等在公共场合欢迎友好团体或个人来访时致辞所用的讲话稿；或者致欢迎信给某人邀请来访。

　　另一个特点是口语性。欢迎词用于口头表达的常常通俗易懂，令人感到亲切。无论是用于书面发表的欢迎词还是口语欢迎词，最好营造出一种现场感。

格式：

欢迎词的基本格式和写法

1）称呼 attendee

2）开头段 First paragraph（开头通常应说明现场举行的是何种仪式，发言者代表什么人向哪些来宾致欢迎词。）

3）主体（主体部分一般阐述和回顾双方在共同的领域里或事业中的共同立场、观点、目标、原则或具体地介绍来宾在各方面的成就和贡献，指出来宾到访对双方的友谊与合作具有何种现实意义。有些欢迎词也可以介绍本单位的情况让来宾对自己有所了解。）

4）结束语（在结尾处通常要再次对来宾表示欢迎、祝愿和感谢。）

书面欢迎词，一般和写信格式相同：日期、称呼、开头、主体、结束语、致词人头衔和姓名。

Useful Expressions

I welcome you with my whole heart/I offer a warm welcome

Please permit me to offer you a(n) ... welcome

We feel honored in offering you a cheerful welcome

On behalf of..., I am delighted to welcome all of you to...

I'm honored to have this opportunity to welcome all of you to ...

May we bid you a sincere welcome ...?

Sample 1:

Dear Guests, Students, Faculty Teachers and Residents,

Please allow me to welcome you sincerely on the occasion of the Second anniversary of the founding of the City Polytechnical University. Although it is relatively young for such an institution, it matches itself to older and renowned universities throughout the world.

Within these two years we have developed nine Bachelor's programs, five of which are already successfully running, and seventeen master's programs, in three of which more than fifty students are studying.

Our university publishing house has already printed its first nine editions of our lecturers. We have already developed numerous partnerships with companies from industry and business, and consolidated our collaboration and co-operation with universities from some Asian countries such as China.

We have organized a scientific conference on the occasion of the first anniversary of the university, and it has become a tradition since then.

Last year, a round table on the topic "New trends and Challenges in Engineering Education" was held. Nineteen students from China, Japan, South Korea took part in the student session, as part of the conference.

As the date of our two-year anniversary has arrived, we can claim to have become a model of the institutional environment of the city. We can help and give it a more academic spirit, and a modern and innovative image. We will keep up this pace and will continue to develop the University. Our goal is for this University to reach the level of the best universities in its academic profile, and to help it become a model of Asian education.

Happy anniversary!

Professor Dalores,
President of City Polytechnical University

Sample 2:

> Dear New Attendee,
>
> A very good evening to all of you and a warm welcome, as we celebrate the eighth anniversary of our "Lifestyle Magazine". It is an exceptional night. Five years ago Fred and I started this magazine in the garage of a friend's house, because frankly, that was all we could afford as an office. It is thanks to all the special people who joined us here today that we are able to celebrate eight years of not just running this magazine, but being successful at it. To all those people who could not join us here today, we miss you.
>
> Tonight though, is about enjoying ourselves. Not looking at tomorrow but celebrating the present, so go ahead and "let your hair down". Have a magical night! You have all worked so hard for it. Surround yourselves with the happiness you deserve and thank you for making this possible.
>
> Smith White

Assignment: *Suppose you are the Dean of the Chemistry Department. You would like to write a letter to welcome a new teacher (Dr. Johnson) to work with.*

Part V Cultural Express

Cross-Cultural Differences

Meeting people from another culture can be difficult. From the beginning, people may send the wrong signal. Or they may pay no attention to signals from another person who is trying to develop a relationship.

Different cultures emphasize the importance of relationship building to a greater or lesser degree. For example, business in some countries is not possible until there is a relationship of trust. Even with people at work, it is necessary to spend a lot of time in "small talk", usually over a glass of tea, before they do any job. In many European countries—like the UK or France—people find it easier to build up a lasting working relationship at restaurants or cafes rather than at the office.

Talk and silence may also be different in some cultures. I once made a speech in Thailand. I had expected my speech to be a success and start a lively discussion; instead there was an uncomfortable silence. The people present just stared at me and smiled. After getting to know their ways better, I realized that they thought I was talking too much. In my own culture, we express meaning mainly through words, but people there sometimes feel too many words are unnecessary.

Even within Northern Europe, cultural differences can cause serious problems. Certainly, English and German cultures share similar values; however, Germans prefer to get down to business more quickly. We think that they are rude. In fact, this is just because one culture starts discussions and makes decisions more quickly.

People from different parts of the world have different values, and sometimes these values are quite against each other. However, if we can understand them better, a multicultural environment (多元文化环境) will offer a wonderful chance for us to learn from each other.

Travel in China

Regardless of the time spent in advance preparation, you are sure to experience a certain amount of cultural shock when you come to travel in China. The more flexible and sensitive you are to the Chinese culture, the more quickly you will be able to adapt. The best way to know a culture is to touch it, to experience it because each culture has its own reasons to exist, and it is hard to say which one is the standard. Confucius once said, reading and traveling are two main ways to obtain knowledge. It would be great since you want to go to China to see it with your own eyes.

In China, the tour guide and his manager are regarded as the same. Nobody is thought of as a servant, so you have to remember: Don't treat any Chinese, especially your guide as a servant! Tour members frequently make personal requests to their guides, which the guide will try their best to satisfy. Sometimes the guide will consult with your tour leader, and the tour leader will explain to you if they cannot satisfy yours. Generally there is little flexibility in the schedule. Your Chinese guide may go to great lengths to avoid saying "No" to a request. Chinese people like to answer a question in an indirect way, so they would say "We shall consider it" instead of "No".

A smile is indeed the universal language. Joining a group, tourists must understand that the guide needs cooperation from each tourist. Your cooperation will be remembered by your tour leader and guide, as well as other tourists. We do suggest you have the experience, and also wish to listen from you what you see, hear and experience in China. You will have many Chinese friends if you are friendly to them.

Unit 5　Culture Shock

拓展词汇

文化

Cutural exchange 文化传播; cultural communication 文化交流; international cultural trade 对外文化贸易; international cultural publicity 对外文化宣传; small-fund aid for cultural development 小额文化援助

宗教

Buddhism 佛教; Judaism 犹太教; Islamism 伊斯兰教; Christianity 基督教(总称,基督教包括基督教新教、天主教、东正教); Protestantism 新教(在中国被称为基督教); Catholicism 天主教; Orthodox 东正教; Hinduism 印度教; Taoism 道教

景点

The Great Wall 长城; Temple of Heaven 天坛; Hutongs and Courtyards in Beijing 北京胡同; the Grand Canal 大运河; Dujiangyan Irrigation Project 都江堰水利工程; the Terra-cotta Warriors and Horses 兵马俑; Longmen Grottos 龙门石窟; Leshan Giant Buddha 乐山大佛; Jiuzhaigou Valley 九寨沟; Mt. Luhan 庐山; Mt. Huangshan 黄山; Confucius Temple 孔庙; Wuhou Temple 武侯祠; Mt.Taishan 泰山; Mt. Emei 峨眉山; Huanglong Valley 黄龙谷; Yin Ruins 殷墟; Water Town of Tongli 同里水乡; Qiao's Compund 乔家大院; Tengwang Tower 滕王阁; Penglai Pavilion 蓬莱阁; Yellow Crane Tower 黄鹤楼; Lingyin Temple 灵隐寺; Former Residence of Chen Yi 陈毅故居; Lu Xun's Memorial Hall 鲁迅纪念馆

工艺品

porcelain 瓷器; chopsticks 筷子; Chinese Fancy Knot 中国结; cloisonnè 景泰蓝; fan 扇子; silk 丝绸; embroidery 刺绣; New Year Painting 年画; Paper cutting 剪纸; festive lantern 花灯; screen tables 屏风; iron picture 铁画; Shadow puppet 皮影; puppet 木偶; kite 风筝; diabolo 空竹; Windmill 风车; clay figurine 泥人

中国传统节日

Spring Festival 春节
Lantern Festival 元宵节
Qingming Festival 清明节
Dragon Boat Festival 端午节
Water-Sprinkling Festival 泼水节
Seventh Evening Festival 七夕
Mid-Autumn Festival 中秋节

Unit 6

Technology and Life

Learning Objectives:

You are able to:
- Talk on the phone
- Understand computers and Internet
- Follow operating instructions
- Write farewell speech/letter

You are suggested to:
- Recognize the English Expressions of technology
- Be familiar with new technological trend

Part I Listening and Speaking

Warm-up

Task 1

Directions: Do you know their Chinese meanings? Try to say something about some of them.

Wi-Fi	GPS	LCD	desktop	laptop
blog	browse	mouse	log onto	account
download	e-commerce	virtual	smart phone	text
message	subscriber	nanotechnology	genetic modification	
Hi-tech				

Task 2

Directions: Do you know the following technological phrases in English? Work with your partner and match them with their English equivalents.

超小型设计 ☆	★ Portable MP3 Digital Audio Player
需要一节五号电池 ☆	★ Built-in 32MB Flash Memory
数字式录音功能 ☆	★ Smart Media Card Slot for Additional Memory
便携式MP3数字放音机 ☆	★ Super Compact Slim Design
嵌入式32兆闪存 ☆	★ Digital Voice Recording Function
点阵液晶显示歌名 ☆	★ Dot-Matrix LCD Display Song Title
微型USBPC接口 ☆	★ Digital Preset EQs
智能多媒体插槽以增加内存容量 ☆	★ Mini USB PC Interface
数字预设均衡器 ☆	★ Require 1 AA Battery

Oral Practice

Task 1

Directions : Read the dialogue and answer the following questions.

Secretary: English Department. Can I help you?
Tom: Good morning. May I speak to Dr. An?
Secretary: One moment, please.
An: Hello, Dr. An here.
Tom: Hello, Dr. An. This is Tom Williams from Miami University.
An: Oh, Tom. You've arrived at Pudong Airport, haven't you?
Tom: Yes, I took the earlier flight.
An: How's your trip?
Tom: Very nice.
An: Would you please wait there and I'll go and pick you up?
Tom: OK. By the way, where will you take me first, the hotel or your department?
An: The hotel, so you can have a little rest first.
Tom: Thank you. Is the hotel far away from your school?
An: No, just a ten-minute walk.
Tom: That's wonderful.
An: See you later.
Tom: See you.

1. Who does Tom want to talk to?
   - ☐ Secretary.
   - ☐ Dr. An.
2. Did Tom arrive early?
   - ☐ Yes.
   - ☐ No.
3. Where will Tom go first?
   - ☐ The Hotel.
   - ☐ The Department.

Task 2

Imagine a woman is calling Mrs. Sato, but she's not in. You are answering the phone. Role play with your partner according to the clues given in the brackets.

You: （电话铃响了，您拿起电话接听。）
Lady: （向对方询问 Mrs. Sato 是否在。）
You: （告诉对方她不在，并询问有什么事情需要转告。）
Lady: （让她转告 Mrs. Sato 给 ABC 公司回电话，并留下电话号码。）
You: （告诉对方她一回来你就转告她。）
Lady: （表示感谢。）
You: （表示客气。）

Listening Practice

Task 1

Directions: Listen to the dialogue and tick (√) in the box at the end of the correct answer.

1. What can be done when shopping online?
   - A. Trying on the clothes you buy. ☐
   - B. Feeling the material you want to buy. ☐
   - C. Buying toys, vegetables and medicines. ☐
2. What is the interesting question from the anti-online-shopper?
   - A. What have you bought online this year? ☐
   - B. When and where do you buy online? ☐
   - C. How do you buy online? ☐
3. Where does the man buy groceries online?
   - A. From Drugstore.com. ☐
   - B. From Homegrocer.com. ☐
   - C. From Amazon.com. ☐
4. In terms of buying online, the man agrees that shopping online is still _____.
   - A. foolish ☐
   - B. complicated ☐
   - C. dangerous ☐

5. What is the woman's attitude towards online shopping?
   A. Positive. ☐
   B. Negative. ☐
   C. We don't know. ☐

Task 2

Directions: In this section you will hear a recorded short passage. The passage will be read three times. You are required to put the missing words or phrases in the numbered blanks according to what you hear.

Answering Machine (留言机)

Answering Machines are very popular in (1) _____. People use answering machines for two reasons. One is to screen calls(来电显示)and the other is to get phone messages when they are not at (2) _____.

When people (3) _____, they use an answering machine to (4) _____ which calls they will or will not answer. They listen to the message as the caller has left it. When they found out who is calling, they can decide whether to (5) _____ the phone or not.

An answering machine can also be used to get a message from someone you want to talk to. The machine takes (6) _____ for you when you are not in and you can (7) _____ it when you get home.

Many people (8) _____ when they have to leave messages on answering machines. Sometimes they (9) _____ their messages before they call. This way they are prepared to (10) _____ if a machine answers.

Task 3

Directions: Listen to the conversation and work in pairs to fill in the form given below.

Date _____ Hour _____
To _____
From _____
Of _____
      Area Code   Phone Number
Phone _____ _____
  ( ) Telephoned   ( ) Returned Call
  ( ) Call Back   ( ) Will Call Again
  ( ) Important   ( ) Urgent
Message _____
_____
Signed _____

Part II Reading

Text A

Before Reading:

1. Can you name some of the advanced technology used in our daily lives?
2. Can you list the advantages and disadvantages of technology?

How Has Technology Changed Our Lives

"*I am enough of an artist to draw freely upon my imagination. Imagination is more important than knowledge. Knowledge is limited. Imagination encircles the world.*" — Albert Einstein

How technology has changed our lives is certainly one of the easiest questions to answer, because the way technology has impacted our lives is evident in every walk of life. Human mind has achieved everything by the power of imagination. It is by virtue of imagination that man has ushered in an age dominated by revolutionary technological developments.

From the day of landing on the moon to a trip to Mars; from the introduction of Microsoft Windows to the inception of 3G and 4G technologies; from tape recorders to Apple iPods; from rarely available landline telephones to abundantly available breed of smartphones (智能手机), QWERTY phones (智能键盘手机) and iPhones; from blogging forums to Internet shopping, technological developments have impacted our lives in a way that it is next to impossible to imagine this world without their presence.

Internet technology has changed our life in numerous ways. The global world trade and business has become faster, easier and more reliable. It is easier to book flights and railway tickets. The bill payment and account related works of every business is easily managed by online facilities.

The impact of technology on education is a classic example of how technology has changed our lives. Computers, PowerPoint presentations and Internet technology have given teaching an altogether different dimension.

Education has become computer dominated in this era and it has gone beyond notebooks and blackboards. Computer education has become an integral part of college education all across the globe, as it is the key to make the students competent enough to meet industry requirements.

If you go through the list of latest developments in technology then you will find that most of them have revolutionized the way we communicate. Websites like Facebook and Twitter have given birth to the concepts of social media marketing. From business networking to personal online dating, communication was never so fast and easy in any century, as it is now.

In the last couple of decades, communication has become amazingly faster, thanks to the Internet that brought email and chatting facilities. Instead of sending letters to their respective destinations, it is easier to send an e-mail to your loved ones.

But we also have to look at some of the negative aspects of technology. Lifestyle habits have changed drastically and nowadays, psychologists are frequently using the term, "Internet addiction" to address certain issues in the lives of people who're constantly glued to their computers. So, if we have to conclude as how technology has changed our lives, then the answer is that it has given us the power to make a difference in our lives by using it wisely. It depends on us, how we use and benefit from it, without getting addicted.

New Words

(标★为A级词汇,标☆为超纲词汇)

encircle	/ɪnˈsɜːk(ə)l/	v.	环绕,包围
★virtue	/ˈvɜːtjuː/	n.	效力,功效
★dominate	/ˈdɒmɪneɪt/	v.	控制,操纵
☆inception	/ɪnˈsɛpʃ(ə)n/	n.	开始,开端
rarely	/ˈrɛːli/	adv.	很少,难得
breed	/briːd/	n.	产生
numerous	/ˈnjuːm(ə)rəs/	adj.	数不清的
account	/əˈkaʊnt/	n.	账目,账户
presentation	/prɛz(ə)nˈteɪʃ(ə)n/	n.	发表,展示,描述
★dimension	/dɪˈmɛnʃ(ə)n/	n.	规模,范围
integral	/ˈɪntɪɡr(ə)l, ɪnˈtɛɡr(ə)l/	adj.	缺一不可的,主要的
★competent	/ˈkɒmpɪt(ə)nt/	adj.	有能力的
drastic	/ˈdrɑːstɪk/	adj.	激烈的
address	/əˈdrɛs/	v.	称呼

Phrases and Expressions

usher in	迎来
every walk of life	各行各业
thanks to	由于
be glued to	（眼睛）紧盯着
benefit from	得益于
get addicted to	上瘾

Proper names

Twitter	推特网
Facebook	脸谱网

Exercises

I. Reading Comprehension

Directions: Circle the right answer for the following questions.

1. What does the word "encircle" mean? (Paragraph 1)
   A. Round.　　　B. Surround.　　　C. Cover.　　　D. Discover.
2. Which gives teaching a different dimension?
   A. Computers.　　　　　　　　　B. PowerPoint presentations.
   C. Internet technology.　　　　　D. All the above.
3. Most of the latest developments in technology have revolutionized the way we _____.
   A. see　　　　B. communicate　　　C. speak　　　D. write
4. Which one of the following statements is not true according to the passage?
   A. Technology has impacted every walk of life.
   B. Computer education has become an integral part of college education.
   C. Lifestyle habits haven't changed drastically with the development of technology.
   D. Technology has given us the power to make a difference in our lives by using it wisely.
5. Those who are constantly glued to their computers are called _____.
   A. computer couch　　　　　　　B. net worm
   C. computer fan　　　　　　　　D. Internet addict

II. Word Usage

Directions: Complete each of the following sentences with the correct form of the italicized word given in the brackets.

1. A _____ (*virtue*) state of war exists between the two countries.
2. Several companies are _____ (*competent*) for the contract.
3. Price tends to _____ (*dominant*) all other considerations.
4. You will be asked to _____ (*presentation*) yourself for interview.
5. Maybe I should consult the _____ (*account*) because my wage is less than last month.
6. The buildings and landscapes are well _____ (*integral*).
7. A square (正方形) is two-_____ (*dimension*).
8. With _____ (*rarely*) exceptions, he does not appear in public now.
9. He is truly a football _____ (*addicted*).
10. When he arrived at the front of the cinema, he was warmly welcomed by the _____ (*usher*).

III. Blank Filling

Directions: Translate the Chinese part of the following sentences with the correct form of the words and expressions in the box.

| imagination | impact | evident | available | reliable |
| thanks to | competent | respective | facility | integral |

1. _____ the great performance by all the actors, the play succeeded. (多亏)
2. Tom came down from Beijing for the meeting and Lisa flew from Guangzhou, and when the meeting was over, they returned to their _____ homes. (各自的)
3. Welcome to our hotel. We are fortunate to have this beautiful _____ to accommodate very special guests. (设施)
4. We are looking for someone who is _____ and hardworking. (可靠的)
5. The environment has a huge _____ on tourism. (影响)
6. He has no _____. (想象力)
7. I think you are _____ to look after the baby (胜任).
8. It has now become _____ to us that a mistake has been made. (显然)
9. Further information is _____ on request. (提供)
10. The arms are _____ parts of the human body. (完整的)

IV. Translation

Directions: Put the following English sentences into Chinese.

1. The human mind has achieved everything by the power of imagination.
2. The impact of technology on education is a classic example of how technology has changed our lives.
3. Computer education has become an integral part of college education all across the globe, as it is the key to make the students competent enough to meet the industry requirements.
4. In the last couple of decades, communication has become amazingly faster, thanks to the Internet which brought email and chatting facilities.
5. It depends on us, how we use and benefit from it, without becoming addicted.

V. True or false

Directions: Decide whether the following statements are true or false according to the text. Write "T" if the statement is true and "F" if it is false.

_____ 1. How technology has changed our lives is certainly one of the easiest questions to answer.
_____ 2. Career education is the key to make the students competent enough to meet the industry requirements.
_____ 3. Computers have become even smaller and somehow more powerful and faster than ever before.
_____ 4. A few of the developments in technology have revolutionized the way we communicate.
_____ 5. Technology has given us the power to make a difference in our lives.

Text B

Before Reading:

1. What do you usually do with your mobile phone?
2. What do you know about the iPad? Do you think it is an innovation of communicative technology?

How did the iPad Change Our Lives?

For iPad owners, their lives must have been changed tremendously after the magic invention was introduced. With the increasing number of people interested in the iPad, people's life is changing in a positive way.

Why is the iPad so attractive?

For example, last year, when someone enjoys the iPad over coffee in public, there will be a lot of curious people wondering what it was. But today everyone has heard of the iPad. More and more people are enjoying this new, innovative product which is gradually changing their lives.

The Apple iPad was described as a "magical innovative" product. It is! From the sale of more than 1,500 million units within 9 months, it has changed many lives.

Every morning, warmed with a cup of

Unit 6   Technology and Life

hot coffee, we may take our iPad to view some news from the internet instead of having to revert to the newspapers or television. We can also write in our blog or reply to e-mails. Unlike the usual way of using the computer, it has become quite easy to use.

It makes our computers extremely jealous. They used to be our most popular office equipment at home, but now, we only think of them when dealing with audio and video material.

Some may say that the iPad is not so useful, for it has no keyboard. Actually, it's quite possible to write articles or blogs with its "virtual" keyboard.

The iPad is also a good resource for the people who do not know how to cook, They can find recipes through the iPad and if utilized properly it can also be a good teaching tool for the kitchen.

Are you feeling tired? Then just listen to some music or play games. The iPad has a large storage capacity for both. It is quite different from the common MP3 players or even the iPod Touch. As for the games, The iPad has made "Plants vs. Zombies" more fun and "Angry Birds" more active! The iPad does add more enjoyment to our daily life.

All the features are included here—news, pictures, games, texts, etc. What's more, we can also enjoy the fun of finger painting on the iPad without all of the mess!

In addition to entertainment, the iPad has changed most people's reading habits. For those who do not like reading paper books, they prefer the iPad eBooks for the joy of changing electronic pages. And thanks to the innovative battery-saving technology, we can enjoy our iPads for many hours.

Believe it or not, the iPad has really changed many aspects of our lives.

New Words

（标★为A级词汇，标☆为超纲词汇）

★tremendously	/trɪˈmendəsli/	adv.	惊人地，巨大地
innovative	/ˈɪnəvətɪv/	adj.	革新的，创新的
★gradually	/ˈgrædjʊəli/	adv.	逐步地，渐渐地
unit	/ˈjuːnɪt/	n.	个体，一组用具
★virtual	/ˈvəːtjʊəl/	adj.	虚拟的

Phrases and Expressions

revert to	回复（旧习惯）
as for	至于
in addition to	除了

Proper names

iPad	苹果平板电脑

Exercises

I. Summary

Directions: Fill in the blanks with the appropriate words according to your understanding.

Nowadays, almost everyone has heard of (1) _____. It is described as an (2) _____ product. It can be used to (3) _____, (4) _____, (5) _____ and of course, make phone calls. It has no keyboard. But we can write articles with its (6) _____ keyboard. The iPad is also a good (7) _____ for the people who do not know how to (8) _____. Besides, it has a large storage of (9) _____ and (10) _____. Believe it or not, the iPad has really changed our lives.

II. Reading Comprehension

Directions: Fill in the blanks of the following two statements according to the text.

1. Many people like the iPad, because _____.
2. Many people prefer the iPad to paper books because _____.

III. Vocabulary & Structures

Directions: Fill in the blanks with the proper expressions in the box.

tremendous	innovative	gradually	daily	revert to
virtual	as for	mess	in addition to	storage

1. _____ the hotel, it was really uncomfortable and miles from the sea.
2. _____ your earlier question, I think we need a second thought.
3. I want to rent a room with large _____ capacity.
4. Things _____ changed.
5. Our deputy manager is the _____ head of the business.
6. _____ the names on the list, there are six other applicants.

7. It makes a _____ change to me.
8. The kitchen is a _____ !
9. The Apple is an _____ firm.
10. The machines are inspected _____.

IV. Translation

Directions: Put the following English sentences into Chinese.

1. For the iPad owners, their lives must have been changed tremendously after the coming of this new tool.
2. More and more persons are enjoying this new innovative product which is changing their lives gradually.
3. Every morning, warmed with a cup of hot coffee, we may take the iPad to view some news from the internet instead of having to revert to the newspapers or television.
4. As for the games, the iPad has made "Plants vs. Zombies" more funny and "Angry Birds" more active!
5. In addition to entertainment, the iPad has changed most people's reading habits.

Part III Strategies

阅读解析(二)

PRETCO(B)中的摘要题主要是识别细节题较多。做这种题目时首先应通读全文,然后根据题目要求寻找所需信息。题干中的有些词就是去文章相应部分寻找的线索。注意答案不能超过3个单词,这就要求我们找到关键词,并剔除与关键词无关的其他词,以确保信息的准确性。

【例】2011年6月实考题

Car Rental (租赁)

Faster Reservation (预订) and Rental Fees

Simply provide your Hertz Club number to speed up the reservation process. And at over 50 locations in the U. S. and Canada, go to Hertz Club Express counters for faster service.

Reduced Rates and Special Offers

Members may receive a special rate on rentals in the U.S., Canada and Europe, and receive a special rate on child seat rentals.

Reserve Specific Brand (品牌) and Model

At 24 major U.S. airport locations, you can choose the brand and model for your weekly and weekend rentals. Only Hertz Club lets you reserve a specific brand and model, like the Ford Mustang. So the car you want is the one you get. Just book your reservation on www.Hertz.com, or by calling 1-800-654-3131.

Car Rental

Way to speed up reservation: by providing your ____46____

Special rates offered to Hertz Club members:

on car rentals in the U.S., ____47____

on ____48____ rentals

Places for reserving a specific brand and model: at 24 major ____49____

Ways of booking: through the Internet or by ____50____

---

(1) 通过 reservation 和 providing 这两个关键词，我们可以在 **Faster Reservation** (预订) **and Rental Fees** 部分里找出答案为 Hertz Club number。

(2) 通过 Special rates 和 in the U.S. 这两个关键词我们可以在 **Reduced Rates and Special Offers** 部分找出答案为 Canada and Europe。

(3) 通过 on _____ rentals 我们可以找出答案为 child seat。

(4) 通过 24 major 这两个关键词，我们可以在 **Reserve Specific Brand**(品牌) **and Model** 部分找出答案为 U.S. airport locations。

(5) 通过 by 这个关键词我们可以找出答案为 calling 1-800-654-3131。

Sample 1:

The business memo (备忘录) is probably the most frequently used communication within a company. It is called an intra-company communication because it is used by people in their own company or organization. They change to letters, however, when they write a message to people who do not work for their company. A memo creates a written record that may or may not be filed, depending on the receiver and the subject. As you know, spoken messages may be understood or forgotten. A memo, however, becomes a record that does much to ensure the complete communication between the sender and the receiver. The standard form of a memo frequently carries a pre-printed series of items: To, From, Date, and Subject. The first two items include the names of the receiver and the sender. A well-written subject line tells the reader the key topic or topics of the memo.

Unit 6   Technology and Life

Business Memo

Function: for communication within a ____1____

Purpose: 1) to keep a ____2____

2) to ____3____ the complete communication

Items involved: 1) Receiver

2) ____4____

3) Date

4) ____5____

Sample 2:

Dear Sir,

　　I am writing to tell you that your latest shipment(装运) of apples is not up to the standard we expected from you. Many of them are bruised(擦伤), and more than half are covered with little spots. They are classed as Grade A, but I think there must have been some mistake, as they are definitely not Grade A apples.

　　We have always been satisfied with the quality of your produce(农产品), which makes this case all the more puzzling. I would be grateful if you could look into the matter. We would be happy to keep the apples and try to sell them at a reduced price, but in that case we would obviously need a credit(部分退款) from you. Alternatively, you could have us send them back and replace them with apples of the right quality. Would you please call to let me know how you want to handle it?

　　　　　　　　　　　　　　　　　　　　　　　　　Yours faithfully,
　　　　　　　　　　　　　　　　　　　　　　　　　Fiona Stockton
　　　　　　　　　　　　　　　　　　　　　　　　　Purchasing Manager

A Letter of Complaint

Produce involved: Grade A ____1____

Causes of complaint:

1. many of the apples are bruised

2. more than half of the apples are covered with ____2____

Suggested solutions:

1. allow to sell at ____3____ and give ____4____, or

2. send them back and replace them with apples of ____5____.

Part IV Applied Writing

Farewell Speech/Letter (欢送词)

欢送词分为二类：一类用于现场口头发表的欢送词；另一类用于书面表达的欢送词。

欢送词的特点主要体现在两个方面：一是惜别的真情流露，二是欢愉有时幽默的格调。两者的结合是写好欢送词的关键问题。

欢送词不易过长。它与欢迎词在分类上大致相同。

欢送词的格式和写法

1) 称呼

2) 开头（说明此时在举行何种欢送仪式，发言人是以什么身份代表什么单位或什么人向宾客表示欢送的。）

3) 主体（主体部分是核心，主要用来回顾双方在访问和合作期间达成了哪些一致意见、取得了哪些突破性进展、合作中取得了哪些成绩、给双方带来了哪些利益。还可以指出双方友谊的性质和价值，双方合作的深远的历史意义等。）欢送词的标题写法与欢迎词大致相同。所不同的是，欢送词可以写得像一篇抒情散文。

4) 结尾

在结尾处再次表示真挚的欢送之情，表达期望再次合作的心愿。

书面欢送词，一般和写信格式相同：日期、称呼、开头、主体、结束语、致词人头衔和姓名。

Useful Expressions

Miss you already. / I miss you already.

See you later. / I'll see you later. / I'll see you later, then.

See you soon. / I'll see you soon. / I'll see you in a little bit.

With all my best thoughts. / With best wishes.

Our visit to China is drawing to a close and we are leaving for Canada shortly.

Thank you for your warm reception and hospitality.

Thanks and best regards.

Bidding you goodbye is really difficult, for you were always a close friend.

We will be keeping in touch, I hope. You can reach me anytime on my phone number or my email.

We really don't know how to thank you. You have been very considerate and helpful.

• Unit 6   Technology and Life •

Sample 1:

Good Evening Everyone!

    I am sure all of us know Ms. Sarah Summers in the Sales Department of our office. She has always been an outstanding employee and it is impossible for anyone not to have heard of her yet. Unfortunately, Sarah has chosen to move out of the city to pursue further education. And I, as the head of the sales department, would like to say a few things about her, to her and all of you here, before she leaves.

    Sarah joined our company right out of college. Though our organization was a little hesitant to hire her for her lack of experience, the company also saw true potential in her. And might I add, she never missed an opportunity to prove us wrong. A highly passionate girl, Sarah has, if anything, greatly contributed to the improvement in the function of the sales department.

    Sarah, we are going to miss you deeply, for the liveliness you brought whenever you entered a room. Replacing you is going to be so difficult. I, on behalf of everyone here, wish you all the luck with your life ahead. We hope to see you shine brighter and achieve what you truly deserve.

Sample 2:

Dear Mr. Johnson,   Nov. 28

    As you already know, this is my last day with Trade Company. I will be joining Shoe Company on Monday. I'm writing this letter as a token of appreciation for the five wonderful years that I have spent with Trade Company.

    I remember my first day of work. I was so nervous and made a hundred silly mistakes. I was sure you were going to fire me instantly. But instead, you didn't even reprimand(训斥) me. You just pretended that nothing had happened and took upon yourself to make sure that I learned the process thoroughly.

    I cannot thank you enough for showing so much faith in me. Honestly, it was your patience and trust that made me excel in my job here. I've made so many friends here, whom I'm going to treasure for the rest of my life.

    As I leave, my heart is filled with hope, but also with a little regret, on having to part with such a wonderful workplace.

    Thank you once again for everything.

                                                                                       Sincerely yours,
                                                                               _____ (signature)

Assignment: *Suppose you are leaving your company. You would like to write a letter to say goodbye to your workmates.*

Part V Cultural Express

What is Intercultural Communication?

Intercultural communication is a form of global communication. It is used to describe the wide range of communication problems that naturally appear within an organization made up of individuals from different religious, social, ethnic, and educational backgrounds. Intercultural communication is sometimes used synonymously with cross-cultural communication. In this sense it seeks to understand how people from different countries and cultures act, communicate and perceive the world around them. Many people in intercultural business communication argue that culture determines how individuals encode messages, what media they choose for transmitting them, and the way messages are interpreted. In fact, it studies situations where people from different cultural backgrounds interact. Aside from language, intercultural communication focuses on social attributes, thought patterns, and the cultures of different groups of people. It also involves understanding the different cultures, languages and customs of people from other countries. Intercultural communication plays a role in social sciences such as anthropology, cultural studies, linguistics, psychology and communication studies. Intercultural communication is also referred to as the basis for international businesses.

German or Global?

The CEO of Siemens announced last week that his priority for his second year in charge would be to improve the 'global diversity' of managers and warned that Germany's competitiveness could be threatened if it failed to do so.

"The management board are all white males. Our top 600 managers are predominantly white German males. We are too one-dimensional," he said in an interview to mark his first year in charge, according to the Financial Times.

He is not alone. Jorma Ollila, while CEO of Nokia, said that his company had to reflect its key markets in the internal diversity of its staff.

Of course, as the FT goes on to point out in its leader, you have to strike a balance. There are many admirable qualities of German companies, such as their reliability and technical prowess; their long-termism, and the consensus between management and workers that has increased competitiveness through wage restraint.

When diversity is encouraged, yet managed and anchored in some common values which everyone understands and shares, it can be powerful indeed. Not just in business, but also in nations.

We have seen how the various "-isms" of the 20th century have resulted in warfare, oppression and economic failure. They have been rooted in the belief that there is an absolute truth or one way of doing things.

Unit 6　Technology and Life

The USA, of course, is the prime example of a nation that has achieved economic success by managing to get a truly diverse set of people to stick, on the whole, to some core beliefs—such as that anyone can succeed, that you can take risks without too much fear of failure, and that you can learn from your mistakes. Outside of this set of beliefs, you are encouraged to be different, and diversity is in general respected.

The USA has not been doing well in the global popularity stakes in recent years, and certainly, in politics, the media and in business, one could say that it may have tried to export its way of doing things rather vigorously.

But in Europe, where countries like the UK, Germany, the Netherlands and Belgium are struggling with questions of national identity, we could learn a lot from the Americans. At least they have had a clear and shared sense of purpose, while encouraging and supporting difference.

Getting the balance between diversity and shared values right is vital for business success in a changing world as well.

拓展词汇

科技

新兴产业 emerging industries;硅谷 Silicon Valley;虚拟现实 virtual reality;宽带技术 broadband technology;超文本传送协议 hypertext transfer protocol(http);无线传输协议 Wireless Transport Protocol(WTP);无线应用协议 Wireless Application Protocol(WAP);加密技术 encryption technology;三维全息图像 three-dimensional holographic image;图标 icon;计算机文化 cyber culture;三维图像 3-D image;搜索引擎 search engine;计算机辅助设计 CAD(Computer-Aided Design);计算机辅助制造 CAM(Computer-Aided Manufacturing);网络交易 networked transaction;电子自由职业经济 e-lance economy;电子货币 e-currency;电子商务 e-commerce;黑客 hacker;智能电话 smart phone;集成电路 integrated circuit;局域网 Intranet;蜂窝通信 cellular communication;芯片 chip;网民 netizen;界面 interface;在线服务 on-line service

Unit 7

Elite Entrepreneurs

Learning Objectives:

You are able to:
- ☞ Recommend new products
- ☞ Negotiate based on quality and quantity
- ☞ Negotiate based on price
- ☞ Comment on products
- ☞ Write an advertisement

You are suggested to:
- ☞ Be familiar with some famous entrepreneurs
- ☞ Discuss with others about products

Unit 7　Elite Entrepreneurs

Part I　Listening and Speaking

Warm-up

Task 1

Directions: Can you recognize these elite entrepreneurs?

Wang Chuanfu	Bill Gates	Konosuke Matsushita
Li Jiacheng	Wang Yongqing	Liu Chuanzhi
John D.Rockefeller	Steve Paul Jobs	Zhang Yin
Jack Welch		

A　　　B　　　C　　　D　　　E

F　　　G　　　H　　　I　　　J

Task 2

Directions: Can you recganize the following vehicle logos? Work with your partner and match the logos with the corresponding car names.

(　)　　(　)　　(　)　　(　)　　(　)

133

( )   ( )   ( )

( )   ( )

A: Mercedes–Benz	B: Volkswagen	C: Ford	D: BMW
E: Toyota	F: Cadillac	G: Buick	H: Audi
I: Mazda	J: Peugeot		

Oral Practice

Task 1

Directions: Read the dialogue and answer the questions.

Tom: Hi, William. Do you know Apple Incorporated?
William: Yes, Apple Incorporated is a well-known computer company in the world.
Tom: And do you know Steve Jobs?
William: Sure. I think everyone knows about him. He was a famous CEO of Apple Incorporated.
Tom: Do you think he is one of the elite people in the world?
William: Of course. Speaking of Apple Incorporated, everybody will remember Jobs' achivements. He invented Macbook, iphone, ipod, ipad, itunes and so on. These products are attractive to all the people around the world.
Tom: Yes, I have an iphone4, I like it very much. It's so convenient for me to surf the internet and query data for my study.
William: Jobs is a very hard-working man, isn't he?
Tom: Yes, Jobs worked hard and made great contribution to human beings. I am incredibly sad to hear he passed away in 2011.
William: When I heard the news, I felt terrible, too.

Unit 7　Elite Entrepreneurs

1. Who do they talk about?
   □ Albert Einstein.　　　　□ Steve Jobs.
2. Where did Steve Jobs work?
   □ In Apple Corporation　　□ In General Motors
3. Why do they admire him?
   □ Because he has made great contribution to human beings
   □ Because he won all kinds of champions.

Task 2

Directions: Suppose you want to buy a car at the car sales market and your partner is a car dealer there. You want to buy an imported, automatic drive car and it should be efficient in fuel economy. Role-play a conversation with your partner. Then reverse roles.

Listening Practice

Task 1

Directions: Listen to the dialogue and tick (√) in the box at the end of the correct answer.

1. The importer wants_____.
   A. to order some tea sets　　　　　　　　　　　□
   B. to order some embroidered products　　　　□
   C. to order some electric appliances　　　　　□

2. The importer wants_____.
   A. the extra large size shirt ——4000 dozen ☐
   B. the extra large size shirt ——3000dozen ☐
   C. the extra large size shirt ——2500 dozen ☐
3. The importer wants_____.
   A. 4500 pieces of the embroidered table-cloth ☐
   B. 3000 pieces of the embroidered table-cloth ☐
   C. 5000 pieces of the embroidered table-cloth ☐
4. The importer wants_____.
   A. 48000 pairs of walking shoes ☐
   B. 58000 pairs of walking shoes ☐
   C. 28000 pairs of walking shoes ☐
5. The importer wants_____.
   A. 120cm x 120cm, 20 wooden cases of the table-cloth ☐
   B. 120cm x 130cm, 2 cases of the table-cloth ☐
   C. 130cm x 120cm, 100 wooden cases of the table-cloth ☐

Task 2

Directions: In this section you will hear a recorded short passage. The passage will be read three times. You are required to put the missing words or phrases in the numbered blanks according to what you hear.

Bill Gates

Bill Gates is the head of (1) _____ Microsoft and one of (2) _____ men. Gates and Paul Allen founded Microsoft (3) _____ , though Allen left the company in 1983. Gates oversaw (4) _____ of the MS-DOS operating system, the Windows operating interface, the Internet Explorer browser, and a multitude of other popular (5) _____ Along the way he gained (6) _____ for fierce competitiveness and aggressive business savvy. During the 1990s rising Microsoft (7) _____ made Gates the world's wealthiest man; his wealth has at times (8) _____ $75 billion, making Gates (9) _____ of the (10) _____ computer geeks of the late 20th century.

Unit 7　Elite Entrepreneurs

Directions: Look at the list of famous entreprises given below. Listen to the dialogues and write down the missing words in the blanks according to what you have heard.

FAMOUS ENTERPRISES	
Wal-Mart Stores (沃尔玛)	Shell Group (壳牌石油)
General Electric (通用电气)	Siemens (西门子)
Hitachi (日立)	Carrefour (家乐福)
Boeing (波音)	Nestle (雀巢)
Hewlett-Packard (惠普)	Unilever (联合利华)
Sinopec (中国石化)	Procter & Gamble (宝洁)
AOL Time Warner (美国在线时代华纳)	Microsoft Corporation (微软集团)

1. A: Do you know something about (1) _____?
   B: (2) _____ is an American-based multinational computer technology corporation that develops, manufactures, licenses, and supports a wide range of software products for computing devices.

2. A: (3) _____, or the China Petroleum and Chemical Corporation is one of the major petroleum companies in China. In 2005 it ranked first in the Top 500 Enterprises of China.
   B: I know, thank you very much.

3. A: Can you list some famous entreprises in retail?
   B: Let me see. (4) _____ in America, (5) _____ in France and (6) _____ in Holland and so on.

4. A: Do you know Jack Welch?
   B: He is a famous CEO in (7) _____.

5. A: Your laser printer is so advanced. What brand is it?
   B: I bought it yesterday. It is made in America, (8) _____.

6. A: What's the relationship between WEA and (9) _____?
   B: It is said that WEA belongs to (10) _____.

Task 3

Directions: Listen to a short passage and fill in the form given below.

Information on Cancellation of an Order

Order: (1) _____
Delivery date: by (2) _____
Reasons for cancellation:
    1. have already reminded you twice by fax, but receive (3) _____
    2. the other side failed to mak (4) _____
Place for the exhibition: (5) _____

New Words and Expressions

purchase	/ˈpəːtʃɪs/	n.	购买;紧握
		vt.	购买;赢得
embroidered	/ɪmˈbrɔɪdə, ɛm-/	adj.	绣花的
discount	/ˈdɪskaʊnt/	n.	折扣;贴现率
		vt.	打折扣;低估;忽视
wooden	/ˈwʊd(ə)n/	adj.	木制的;僵硬的,呆板的
appliance	/əˈplʌɪəns/	n.	器具;器械;装置
device	/dɪˈvʌɪs/	n.	装置;策略;图案
negotiation	/nɪgəʊʃɪˈeɪʃ(ə)n/	n.	谈判;转让;顺利的通过
laser	/ˈleɪzə/	n.	激光
petroleum	/pɪˈtrəʊlɪəm/	n.	石油
enterprise	/ˈɛntəˌprʌɪz/	n.	企业

Part II Reading

Text A

Before Reading:

1. Are you familiar with some car brands in the Ford Motor Company? Can you name some of them?
2. Are you interested in driving a car? Why or why not?

Unit 7   Elite Entrepreneurs

Henry Ford — Founder of the Ford Motor Company

The competitor to be feared is one who never bothers about you at all, but goes on making his own business better all the time.
— *Henry Ford*

Henry Ford was not the inventor of the automobile, but his innovations in assembly-line skills and the introduction of one-sized changeable parts produced the first mass-production automobile manufacturing plant, paving the way for the cheap automobiles that turned the United States into a nation on wheels.

Ford made several attempts to start his company. In 1903 with $28,000, eleven men, and Ford as Vice President and Chief Engineer, Ford Motor Company was formed. They produced only three cars a day and had up to three men working on each. In 1908 the company produced the famous Model T, a reliable and inexpensive car for the mass market. Ford drove and raced this car at every opportunity to prove how reliable it was. By 1918, half of all cars in the U.S. were a Model T.

In response to growing demand, Ford built a new factory using one-sized

Ford Model T

changeable parts and a conveyor-belt based assembly line. The factory was able to build a car in just 93 minutes, producing around 1 million cars a year. With this advancement in production, Ford was able to market to the general public. The factory had everything it needed to build the cars including a steel mill, glass factory, and the first automobile assembly line.

Ford was also responsible for cutting the workday from nine hours to eight hours, so that the factory could change to a three-shift workday and operate 24 hours a day. When work on the assembly line proved very boring he doubled the wage to $5. There started $5 minimum wages.

In the 1920s, General Motors and

139

Ford Model A

Ford V-8 (racing car)

Ford V8

others began offering cars in a variety of colors with added features, extending credit so that consumers could afford them. Ford insisted on keeping costs down by offering limited features and just one color, black. But after losing market to General Motors, the company shut down for several months to change to the redesigned Model A. After this Ford came out with the "V-8." The vehicles were very successful but the company remained outsold by General Motors.

Ford's main contribution to the Industrial Revolution is the assembly line. He died on April 7, 1947 and his authority was passed down to his grandson Henry Ford II. Today Ford Motor Company is one of the world's leading consumer companies for automotive products, including a family of widely-recognized brands: Ford, Lincoln, Mercury, Mazda, Jaguar, Land Rover, Aston Martin, and Volvo. The Henry Ford Museum in Greenfield Village, a small town in which Ford supported innovation, is one of America's top history attractions.

(462 words)

New Words

（标★为A级词汇，标☆为超纲词汇）

★competitor	/kəmˈpɛtɪtə/	n.	竞争者；对手
★automobile(auto)	/ˈɔːtəməbiːl/	n.	汽车
innovation	/ɪnəˈveɪʃ(ə)n/	n.	改革，创新；新观念
☆assembly-line	/əˈsɛmbli/ /laɪn/		流水线
mass-production	/mas/ /prəˈdʌkʃ(ə)n/		大规模生产
☆manufacture	/ˌmænjʊˈfæktʃə/	v.	制造，生产
attempt	/əˈtɛm(p)t/	n.	试图；尝试
reliable	/rɪˈlaɪəb(ə)l/	adj.	可靠的；可信赖的

Unit 7　Elite Entrepreneurs

inexpensive	/ˌɪnɪkˈspɛnsɪv/	adj.	不贵的,便宜的
response	/rɪˈspɒns/	n.	反应;回答,答复
☆conveyor-belt	/kənˈveɪə/ /bɛlt/		带式运输机
advancement	/ədˈvɑːnsm(ə)nt/	n.	进步;提升
shift	/ʃɪft/	n.	替换,更换
★minimum	/ˈmɪnɪməm/	adj.	最少的;最小的(添加的A级词汇)
feature	/ˈfiːtʃə/	n.	特征,特点
insist	/ɪnˈsɪst/	v.	坚持
outsold	/aʊtˈsəʊld/		卖得比……多 (outsell的过去式和过去分词)
★authority	/ɔːˈθɒrɪti/	n.	权力(替换成了A及词汇)
automotive	/ˌɔːtəˈməʊtɪv/	adj.	自动的;汽车的
widely-recognized	/ˈwʌɪdli/ /ˈrekəɡnʌɪzd/		广泛识别的

Phrases and Expressions

not only ... but also...	不但……而且……
pave the way	为……铺平道路,为……创造条件
attempt to	企图,打算
in response to	……的反应,回应
be responsible for	为……负责
insist on	坚持
shut down	使关闭,停业
contribution to	……的贡献
pass down to	把……传给后世

Proper Names

Henry Ford	亨利·福特,福特汽车公司的创始人
Ford Motor Company	福特汽车公司
General Motors	通用汽车公司
Ford, Lincoln, Mercury, Mazda, Jaguar, Land Rover, Aston Martin, and Volvo	福特汽车公司生产的各种牌子的汽车：福特,林肯,水星,马自达,美洲虎,路虎,阿斯顿·马丁,沃尔沃

Exercises

I. Reading Comprehension

Directions: Circle the right answer for the following questions.

1. Who was Henry Ford?
    A. He was a famous director.
    B. He was an inventor of electronic.
    C. He was an investor.
    D. He was an inventor of automobiles.
2. When was the famous Model T produced?
    A. In 1903.
    B. In 1908.
    C. In 1918.
    D. In 1920.
3. What innovation was Ford responsible for?
    A. The factory could change to a three-shift workday.
    B. The factory could operate 24 hours a day.
    C. He started the $5minimun wage.
    D. A, B and C.
4. Which one of the following statements is correct according to the features of the Model T?
    A. It's an expensive car for the market.
    B. It has a variety of colors.
    C. It's a reliable but inexpensive car for the mass market.
    D. It's a modern and fashion car for the general public.
5. Which one of the following statements is not true according to the text?
    A. Ford's main contribution to the Industrial Revolution is the assembly line.
    B. In 1903 with $28,000, eleven men, Ford Motor Company was formed.
    C. He extended credit so that consumers could afford them.
    D. Ford's innovations paved the way for the cheap automobiles that turned the US into a nation on wheels.

II Word Usage

Directions: Complete each of the following sentences with the correct form of the italicized word given in the brackets.

1. He _____ *(attempt)* to leave but was stopped.
2. Her temper is _____ *(change)*.
3. Who's _____ *(response)* for this terrible mess?
4. If our industries shy away from _____ *(innovate)*, we will never be able to compete successfully with other countries.

5. The _____ (operate) of a new machine can be hard to learn.
6. The idea of traveling to the moon holds little _____ (attract) for me.
7. He has made an important _____ (contribute) to the company.
8. Over 250 cars _____ (produce) by the workers a week.
9. Despite the danger, she _____ (remain) calm.
10. The booklet _____ (offer) practical advice for people with housing problems.

III. Blank Filling

Directions: Translate the Chinese part of the following sentences with the correct form of the words and expressions in the box.

turn into	in response to	up to	pave the way for
not only ... but also...	come out	contribute to	
shut down	pass down to	insist on	

1. _____ can sleep in this tent. (至多十个人)
2. We should _____ lasting peace. (为和平铺平道路)
3. Shakespeare was _____. (不仅是作家，而且还是演员)
4. The whole company _____ for three weeks. (关闭)
5. _____ as soon as it was dark. (星星就出来了)
6. She opened the door _____. (听到敲门声)
7. She _____ the discussion. (根本没起作用)
8. Tom's father _____ to his son. (把他的公司传给了他儿子)
9. _____ when it freezes. (水变成冰)
10. They are _____ repayment immediately. (坚持)

IV. Translation

Directions: Put the following English sentences into Chinese.

1. Ford made several attempts to start his company.
2. In 1908, the company produced the famous Model T, a reliable and inexpensive car for mass market.
3. In response to growing demand, Ford built a new factory using one-sized changeable parts and a conveyor-belt based assembly line.
4. Today Ford Motor Company is one of the world's leading consumer companies for automotive products.
5. Ford's main contribution to the Industrial Revolution is the assembly line.

V. True or False

Directions: Decide whether the following statements are true or false according to the text. Write "T" if the statement is true and "F" if it is false.

_____ 1. By 1918, half of all cars in the US were a V-8.

_____ 2. Ford was responsible for cutting down the workday from nine hours to eight hours.

_____ 3. After losing market share to General Motors, the company changed to the redesigned Model A.

_____ 4. In the 1920s, Ford Motor Company offered cars in a variety of colors.

_____ 5. Henry Ford passed his company down to his son.

Text B

Before Reading:

1. *What are the most famous films or TV productions made by Huayi Brothers?*
2. *Can you list some famous actors, actresses or directors in Huayi Brothers?*

Huayi Brothers and the New Business of Chinese Blockbusters

The entrepreneur Wang Zhongjun can claim to have played a key role in the revolution of entertainment in China. In the mid-1990s, he and his brother Wang Zhonglei founded a small company that has now grown into one of China's largest media corporations. Its business includes film and TV production and distribution.

Wang Zhongjun began his career in art and graphic design, and he spent several years living and working in the US. On his return to China, he became interested in the idea of starting an advertising agency. He could not get any help with start-up capital, so he and his brother invested their savings in the venture.

In order to create a good impression for prospective clients and investors, he rented a big office and hired 30 staff — despite the fact that he only had enough money to pay his employees for six months.

The breakthrough for the company came about in a surprising way. One day, Wang Zhongjun remembered the signs advertising the McDonalds hamburger chain that he'd seen almost everywhere in America.

He wondered whether he could bring

the Western approach to branding in China, and offer professional-looking signs to Chinese businesses. But he discovered that the signs used to advertise shops and restaurants in the US were made of high quality materials that seemed to be difficult to obtain in China.

Another problem was there didn't seem to be many chain stores in China, which might have been the best potential customers. However there were a number of Chinese banks with lots of branches, so Mr. Wang decided to concentrate on these.

He imported raw materials, and set up facilities to make the signs, while at the same time continuing negotiations with prospective clients. He ended up focusing on one main customer, which helped to keep the company busy for almost two years.

When the firm had capital to expand in the late 1990s it moved into TV and film production. The company hired some of China's best-known directors to make its first few films. Although they didn't make much money at this stage, the success of the films helped to establish their reputation in the industry. Since then the company has gone on to make more than 30 movies, making hundreds of millions of dollars.

In China there is strict official censorship of movies. But Wang Zhongjun does not think it is an obstacle. He points out that to a certain degree, film censorship exists in many countries around the world. It's important for all businesses to understand and abide by the regulations, controlling the industry they operate in and movie-making is no different.

A bigger concern for him is whether they can actually succeed in producing movies that will appeal to audiences. The key to this lies in maintaining good relations with the producers, directors and acting talents at the heart of the creative process.

Wang Zhongjun believes that there are good prospects for future expansion for the entertainment industry in China, particularly if the strong economic growth in the country and the Asia-Pacific region continues. He wants his company to take full advantage of the opportunities ahead; his dream is for Huayi Brothers to become "a film-making giant".

New Words

(标★为A级词汇,标☆为超纲词汇)

词	音标	词性	释义
☆blockbuster	/ˈblɒkbʌstə/	n.	重磅炸弹,了不起的人或事;大片;风靡一时的事物
entrepreneur	/ˌɒntrəprəˈnɜː/	n.	企业家
★corporation	/ˌkɔːpəˈreɪʃ(ə)n/	n.	公司;法人
distribution	/ˌdɪstrɪˈbjuːʃ(ə)n/	n.	(电影在各院线的)发行,上映
graphic	/ˈgrafɪk/	adj.	图解的,用图表示的
invest	/ɪnˈvɛst/	v.	投资

★venture	/ˈvɛntʃə/	n.	商业冒险
☆prospective	/prəˈspɛktɪv/	adj.	未来的
investor	/ɪnˈvɛstə/	n.	投资者
concentrate	/ˈkɒns(ə)ntreɪt/	v.	专心于；注意
facility	/fəˈsɪlɪti/	n.	设备；设施
★negotiation	/nɪgəʊʃɪˈeɪʃ(ə)n/	n.	协商，谈判（negotiate v.）
☆censorship	/ˈsɛnsəʃɪp/	n.	审查制度
abide	/əˈbʌɪd/	v.	遵守
★regulation	/rɛgjʊˈleɪʃ(ə)n/	n.	管理；控制；规章；规则（添加的A及词汇）
region	/ˈriːdʒ(ə)n/	n.	地区；区域
giant	/ˈdʒʌɪənt/	n.	巨人

Phrases and Expressions

take advantage of	利用；欺骗
play a key role in	起着重要的作用
set up	建立，准备；安排
focus on	注重
abide by	遵守，遵照（法规、约定等）

Proper Names

| Huayi Brothers (Media Corporation) | 华谊兄弟传媒股份有限公司 |
| Asia-Pacific region | 亚太地区 |

Exercises

I. Summary

Directions: Fill in the blanks with the appropriate words according to your understanding.

The entrepreneur Wang Zhongjun have played a key role in the revolution of (1) _____ in China. In the mid-1990s, he and his brother Wang Zhonglei founded a small company that has now grown into one of China's largest (2) _____ corporations. Its business includes (3) _____ and TV production and (4) _____. The success of the films helped to establish their (5) _____ in the industry. Wang Zhongjun believes that there are good (6) _____ for future expansion for the (7) _____ industry in China, particularly if the strong (8) _____ growth in the country and the Asia-Pacific region continues. He wants his company to take full advantage of the (9) _____ ahead; his dream is for Huayi Brothers to become "a (10) _____ giant".

Unit 7 Elite Entrepreneurs

II. Reading Comprehension

Directions: Fill in the blanks of the following two statements according to the text.

1. Wang Zhongjun believes whether they can actually succeed in producing movies that will appeal to _____. The key to this lies in maintaining good relations with the producers, _____ and acting talents at the heart of the creative process.
2. _____ is important for all businesses to understand and abide by the regulations controlling the industry they operate in and movie-making is no different.

III. Vocabulary & Structures

Directions: Fill in the blanks with the proper expressions in the box.

agency	appeal to	concentrate on	giant
end up	breakthrough	take advantage of	point out
invest	abide by		

1. They have found a major _____ in the treatment of cancer.
2. I got this job through an employment _____.
3. We didn't like it at first, but we _____ cheering.
4. You must _____ the consequences of your decision.
5. You should _____ the fine weather to repair the house.
6. Carol _____ $1000 in an oil company.
7. Honda is a _____ car in the international market.
8. This year the company _____ improving its efficiency.
9. The government _____ everyone to save water.
10. May I _____ that if we don't leave now we shall miss the bus?

IV. Translation

Directions: Put the following English sentences into Chinese.

1. The entrepreneur Wang Zhongjun can claim to have played a key role in the revolution of entertainment in China.
2. On his return to China, he became interested in the idea of starting an advertising agency.
3. The breakthrough for the company came about in a surprising way.
4. He discovered that the signs used to advertise shops and restaurants in the US were made of high quality materials that seemed to be difficult to obtain in China.
5. A bigger concern for him is whether they can actually succeed in producing movies that will appeal to audiences.

Part III Strategies

阅读解析（三）

匹配题主要考查学生对英文标识语和某一领域的专业术语的识别能力以及学生查阅列表和目录的能力。测试的内容具有较强的应用性，如：各种列表，公共场所的标志用语等。题目以单词或短语形式出现，其中英文术语多，中文术语少。学生答题时可根据题目中的中文找出相对应的英文选项，也可以根据英文寻找相对应的中文选项。

【例】2011年6月实考题

 A. courses taken   B. current address
 C. date of birth   D. educational background
 E. email address   F. health conditions
 G. hobbies and interests   H. ID card No.
 I. on-the-job training   J. job objective
 K. permanent address   L. marital status
 M. part-time jobs   N. position applied for
 O. rewards   P. scholarships
 Q. work experience

Examples: (L) 婚姻状况   (H) 身份证号码

 51.（ ）兼职工作   （ ）工作经历
 52.（ ）工作目标   （ ）教育程度
 53.（ ）健康状况   （ ）在职培训
 54.（ ）所学课程   （ ）兴趣爱好
 55.（ ）申请职位   （ ）目前地址

这道题中的短语主要与求职招聘有关。中文意思如下：
 A. 所学课程   B. 目前地址   C. 出生日期   D. 教育程度
 E. 邮箱地址   F. 健康状况   G. 兴趣爱好   H. 身份证号码
 I. 在职培训   J. 工作目标   K. 常用地址   L. 婚姻状况
 M. 兼职工作   N. 申请职位   O. 获奖情况   P. 奖学金
 Q. 工作经验

答案为：51.（M)(Q)   52.（J)(D)   53.（F)(I)   54.（A)(G)   55.（N)(B)

Self-practice Exercise:

A. adjustment letters
B. annual reports
C. risk management
D. trade fair
E. feasibility reports
F. holding company
G. operating costs
H. quality specification
I. inside packaging
J. irrevocable credit
K. corporate restructuring
L. financial management
M. reference letters
N. technology transfer
O. intellectual property rights
P. knowledge-based economy
Q. performance-related pay

Examples: (P) 知识经济　　　(K) 公司重组

1. (　) 交易市场　　　(　) 风险管理
2. (　) 投诉回复函　　(　) 可行性报告
3. (　) 技术转让　　　(　) 不可撤销信用证
4. (　) 营业成本　　　(　) 质量标准
5. (　) 控股公司　　　(　) 内包装

Part IV Applied Writing

Advertisement（广告）

广告故名词义就是广而告之。是借助广播、电视、报刊以及网络，通过文字、图象和声音来宣传、介绍和推销自己的产品和服务，扩大产品的影响，促进产品销售的一种宣传方式。广告词指的是广告作品中用以表达广告主题和创意的全部语言，要求语言简洁凝炼、通俗易懂、新颖独特、富有情趣、主题突出。广告传播的方式多种多样，有电视广告、平面广告、广播广告等。

广告的格式：

一般包括标题、正文、随文三大基本部分。

1) 标题

标题是招牌，用来吸引人们或顾客的关注和好奇心。标题不能偏离内容。它在全篇的广告词中有着十分重要的作用。标题一般短小而简练。

2) 正文

正文是广告词的中心和主体。在正文里必须体现广告的目的和内容，在正文部分，要摆出强有力的证据来说明商品的优越性。不要转弯抹角。避免无限夸张、无特色。要具体真实,使话语具有诱惑力。正文应该多长,取决于产品。广告必须是你产品的完整推销广告。好的广告会成为百姓交谈惯用口语。

3) 随文

　　随文的作用是方便消费者联系购买,一般包括厂名、厂址、电话(传真)号码等,必要时还可写上开户银行、银行账户以及购销方法等。

　　广告英语的语体特点:独撰新词或拟音拼写(Coinage or homophone);频繁使用形容词(Adjective),灵活运用复合词(Compounds);多用简单句和省略句(Simple sentences and elliptical clauses),常用疑问词和祈使句(Interrogative sentences and imperative sentences);用拟人(Personification)、比喻(Anology)、双关(Pun)、反复(Repetion)等修辞手段。

　　需要指出的是广告的创意和制作既要讲求新颖、别致,让人过目不忘,又要考虑公众欣赏习惯,遵守国家有关法令。要反对误导公众、贻害社会的虚假广告、不洁广告,在充分发挥广告的经济效益的同时,注意其不容忽略的社会文化效应。

Sample 1

WUHAN TRANSLATION CENTER(TWC)
OPENING A NEW CHANNEL OF COMMUNICATION

With a staff of highly-qualified translators, WTC guarantees satisfaction with its prompt services.

WTC's business scope includes: Translation, into and from Chinese, of books, documents, historical data, advertisement, contracts, rules and regulations, and teaching materials.

The service is provided in various languages.
Address: RM105 Hongshan Hotel, 345 Hongshan Road ,Wuhan
Tel: 027-88352599
Fax: 88352925

Sample 2

Oats–Walnut Powder—A Delicious Drink
Packed by
China National Grain, Oils &Food
Import &Export Corporation, Guilin

Oats-Walnut Powder, a well-known beverage exported by this corporation, is prepared from Glucose, Malt Extract, Condensed Milk, Cocoa, Sesame, Oats, Walnut, egg and Granulated Sugar.

It contains many nutrients necessary for human health and is specially fortified with Vitamins A, B and C. Being easily digestible and helping to increase appetite. Oats-Walnut Powder is recommended as the best daily energy drink of its kind.

Oats-Walnut Powder may be served hot or cold as you like. A delicious and nutritious drink can be made in an instant simply by placing two or three table spoons (about 30g) of Oats-Walnut Powder in a cup or glass, adding boiling water or milk and stirring well to dissolve.

Ingredients of Oats-Walnut Powder:

Protein: 7%-9%   Fat: 10%-14%
Total Carbohydrate: 65%-70%
Mineral Substances: 1%-2.5%
Moisture: 25%Max
Each 120g of Oats-Walnut Powder Contains
Vitamin A: 1800I.U
VitaminB1: 1.8mg
Vitamin C: 1200I.U

Assignment: *Write an advertisement according to the information given below:*

台式电风扇

最新的遥控和程控设计

胜美牌系列电风扇装备有最新的集成电路AS9201,拥有最先进的程控设计。

3种风速选择:午休时给你阵阵自然凉风;瞌睡时,给你微风助你入睡,在你设定的时刻自动停止。

15种时间和速度选择:从半小时到七个半小时不等。

规格:

额定电压:220伏   交流电:50赫兹

用电量:46瓦

重量:6公斤

制造商:深圳先科机电公司
地址:中国深圳八卦东四路
电话:2264453
(程控设计:program and the latest formula in the industry
  集成电路:integrated circuit   额定电压:rated voltage)

Part V Cultural Express

Microsoft Corporation

Microsoft Corporation is an American-based multinational computer technology corporation that develops, manufactures, licenses, and supports a wide range of software products for computing devices. Headquartered in Redmond, Washington, USA, its best selling products are the Microsoft Windows operating system and the Microsoft Office suite of productivity software.

Originally founded to develop and sell BASIC interpreters for the Altair 8800, Microsoft rose to dominate the home computer operating system market with MS-DOS in the mid-1980s, followed by the Windows line of operating systems. Its products have all achieved near-ubiquity in the desktop computer market. One commentator notes that Microsoft's original mission was "a computer on every desk and in every home, running Microsoft software". Microsoft possesses footholds in other markets, with assets such as the MSNBC cable television network, the MSN Internet portal, and the Microsoft Encarta multimedia encyclopedia. The company also markets both computer hardware products such as the Microsoft mouse as well as home entertainment products such as the Xbox, Xbox 360, Zune and MSN TV. The company's initial public stock offering was in 1986; the ensuing rise of the company's stock price has made four billionaires and an estimated 12,000 millionaires from Microsoft employees.

Throughout its history the company has been the target of criticism, including monopolistic business practices and anti-competitive business practices including refusal to deal and tying. The U.S. Justice Department and the European Commission, among others, have ruled against Microsoft for various antitrust violations.

Known for what is generally described as a developer-centric business culture, Microsoft has historically given customer support over Usenet newsgroups and the World Wide Web, and awards Microsoft MVP status to volunteers who are deemed helpful in assisting the company's customers.

拓展词汇

高层技术和管理人员

boss 老板；manager 经理；supervisor 监督者；advisor 顾问或者导师；specialist 专家；consultant 顾问；team leader 团队领导；founder 创始人；contractor 承包人；president 总裁，董事长；chief executive officer 执行总裁，首席执行官；chairmen 主席；owner 物主；director 主管，主任；employer 雇主；assistant manager 经理助理；senior manager 资深经理；senior engineer 高级工程师；project manager 项目经理

企业运作和管理

offer 出价；order（下）订单；contract 合同；negotiation 谈判；procurement 采购；assets evaluation 资产评估；overhead 管理费；profit 利润；purchase order 采购单；taxation 税务；warehouse 仓库；welfare 福利；capital 资金；registered capital 注册资本；bank account 银行往来帐；feasibility report 项目可行性报告

Unit 8

Failure and Success

Learning Objectives:

You are able to:
- ☞ Offer congratulations
- ☞ Accept congratulations and express gratitude
- ☞ Give comfort and encouragement
- ☞ Comment on failures and successes
- ☞ Write a memo

You are suggested to:
- ☞ Recognize the slogans of some brands
- ☞ Learn about a few successful corporations

• Unit 8 Failure and Success •

Part I Listening and Speaking

Warm-up

Task 1

Directions: Do you know their names? Please say something about these famous figures, their failures and successes.

Abraham Lincoln	Thomas Edison	Liu Xiang	Madame Curie
Sylvester Stallone	Li Na	Deng Xiaoping	
Ludwig Van Beethoven			

(1) (2) (3) (4)

(5) (6) (7) (8)

155

Task 2

Directions: Can you match the following brand logos with the slogans?

1. Good to the last drop.
2. Feel the new space.
3. Impossible is nothing.
4. Obey your thirst.
5. Intelligence everywhere.
6. When there's no tomorrow.
7. Think different.
8. The best a man can get.
9. The ultimate driving.
10. Melt in your mouth — not in your hand.

Oral Practice

Task 1

Directions: Read the dialogue and answer the following questions.

Mary: What a game! You played a perfect game today, John. Many congratulations on winning the championship!

John: Thank you very much for saying so. I can hardly believe we won the championship.

Mary: You folks deserved it, especially you. You were the highest scorer of all. I really feel happy for you.

John: Thanks. Still, basketball is a team sport. The guys all worked hard for this day.

Mary: That's true. I think this calls for a big celebration.

John: Oh, yes. The school is planning a party for us next Monday.

Mary: I can't wait for the celebration! I bet the whole school is excited!

1. Why did John receive congratulations?
   ☐ Winning a scholarship.   ☐ Winning a championship.
2. In what sport did they win a championship?
   ☐ Basketball.   ☐ Football.
3. How will they celebrate it?
   ☐ To have a drink together.   ☐ To hold a party.

Task 2

Directions: Suppose you are Joe, managing director of the Marketing Department. You've just received a congratulation card from your friend Carol for your promotion. Now you're talking with her to express your appreciation. Role-play a conversation with your partner. Then reverse roles.

Dear Joe,

It was a pleasure to hear that you were promoted to the position of managing director in the Marketing Department. My heartiest congratulations!

I really think you deserve the position after years of service and experience you have had in this field.

You have my best wishes for your greater success in all that you undertake.

Sincerely yours,
Carol

Listening Practice

Task 1

Directions: Listen to the dialogues and tick (√) in the box at the end of the correct answer.

1. The man feels _____ about the class.
    A. good ☐
    B. terrible ☐
    C. crazy ☐
2. The son feels _____ after hearing the news.
    A. depressed ☐
    B. sad ☐
    C. excited ☐
3. They are talking about _____.
    A. finishing a project ☐
    B. practicing oral English ☐
    C. playing the piano ☐
4. The man congratulates the woman on _____.
    A. winning the first prize ☐
    B. winning the silver medal ☐
    C. winning the championship ☐
5. They will celebrate Mike's promotion by _____.
    A. having a drink ☐
    B. holding a party ☐
    C. going to the cinema ☐

Task 2

Directions: In this section you will hear a recorded short passage. The passage will be read three times. You are required to put the missing words or phrases in the numbered blanks according to what you hear.

  I have thought so much through these (1) _____ experiences about how I have grown and learned from them. I stay positive and (2) _____ get down I just move forward and get excited for what's next. I figure that things didn't (3) _____ because they just weren't the right fit. I have a friend who keeps (4) _____ me about the story of the fish who keeps trying to (5) _____ a tree and fails...because they're a fish! I'm trying to (6) _____ what I'm good at, what I'm supposed to be doing so that I end up in the right (7) _____ and with a career or maybe a few different jobs or projects that use the skills I've been given. I'll recognize (8) _____ when I know that I'm in the right place doing what I'm good at. The failures are just another (9) _____ and in the end it isn't failure and success.

  Thanks for failures, because without them, you wouldn't be who you are today and wouldn't be able to (10) _____ them with others.

Task 3

Directions: Listen to the conversation and work in pairs to fill in the blanks given below.

1. Peter congratulates Joan on her appointment as _____ of the department.
2. Peter thinks she is the _____ person for the job both in terms of _____ and _____.
3. Joan hopes she can still count on Peter's _____ and _____.
4. Joan used to work as an _____.
5. Joan likes the job because it can give full play to her _____.

Part II Reading

Text A

Before Reading:

1. *Do you know the person in the pictures? What do you think of his death?*
2. *Some successful people once dropped out of college, such as Steve Jobs and Bill Gates. What's your opinion about it?*

Looking Back and Looking Forward

I dropped out of Reed College after the first 6 months. Why? The reason started before I was born. My biological mother was a college graduate. She did not marry then, so she decided to put me up for adoption. She felt strongly that I should be adopted by college graduates, so I was to be adopted at birth by a lawyer and his wife. Then my parents got a call asking: "We have a baby boy; do you want him?" They said: "Of course." My biological mother later found out that my adoptive parents had never got a very good education and so she refused to sign the final adoption papers until my parents promised that I would someday go to college.

And 17 years later I did go to college, but I chose a very expensive one and all of my working-class parents' savings were being spent on my tuition. After six months, I couldn't see the value in it, so I decided to drop out and trust that it would all turn out well in the end. It was pretty terrible at the time, but looking back it was one of the best decisions I ever made. The minute I dropped out I could stop taking the required classes that didn't interest me, and begin dropping in on the ones that looked interesting.

It wasn't all romantic. I didn't have a dorm room, so I slept on the floor in friends' rooms. I returned coke bottles for 5¢ to buy food with. However much of what I came upon then turned out to be priceless later on.

Reed College at that time offered perhaps the best calligraphy instruction in the country. Because I had dropped out, I decided to take a calligraphy class to learn how to do this. It was beautiful and historical in a way that science can't show, and I found it interesting. At that time, I never had a hope of ever using calligraphy in my life. But ten years later, when we were designing the first computer, it all came back to me. If I had never dropped out, I would have never dropped in on this calligraphy class, and personal computers might not have the wonderful typography that they do now. Looking back, this was really a valuable experience for me. Of course it was impossible to connect the dots looking forward when I was in college. But it was very, very clear looking backwards ten years later.

Again, you can't connect the dots looking forward; you can only connect them looking backwards. So you have to trust that the dots will somehow connect in your future. You have to trust in something — your courage, destiny, life, whatever. This approach has never let me down, and it has made all the difference in my life.

(477 words)

New Words

（标★为A级词汇，标☆为超纲词汇）

★biological	/ˌbaɪəˈlɒdʒɪkl/	adj.	亲生的；有血缘关系（而不是领养关系）
★adoption	/əˈdɒpʃn/	n.	收养；领养
★adopt	/əˈdɒpt/	v.	收养；领养
graduate	/ˈɡrædʒuət/	n.	毕业生
tuition	/tjuˈɪʃn/	n.	学费
romantic	/rəʊˈmæntɪk/	adj.	罗曼蒂克的；富于浪漫色彩的；有浪漫情调的
priceless	/ˈpraɪsləs/	a.	无价的；无法估价的；贵重的
calligraphy	/kəˈlɪɡrəfi/	n.	书法；美术字
instruction	/ɪnˈstrʌkʃn/	n.	教学；讲授；教授；指导
typography	/taɪˈpɒɡrəfi/	n.	印刷版面式样
dot	/dɒt/	n.	点
destiny	/ˈdestəni/	n.	命运
approach	/əˈprəʊtʃ/	n.	途径；方式；方法；态度；处理

• Unit 8 Failure and Success •

Phrases and Expressions

drop out	退学;退出
turn out	结果(是);证明(是);最终是
let (sb.) down	使失望;辜负
make a difference	有关系;有影响;起(重要)作用

Exercises

I. Reading Comprehension

Directions: Circle the right answer for the following questions.

1. The author's biological mother didn't intend to bring him up herself because _____.
   A. She had no money.
   B. She was not married.
   C. She didn't know how to raise a child.
   D. She didn't like a child.

2. On what condition did the author's biological mother agree to sign the adoption paper?
   A. The baby would go to college.
   B. The baby's adopted parents must be college graduates.
   C. The baby's adopted parents must be very rich.
   D. The baby's adopted parents must be Americans.

3. The author dropped out of college because _____.
   A. he wasn't interested in the courses he took.
   B. he couldn't pay for the tuition.
   C. he didn't like his college.
   D. he didn't like his teachers.

4. What did the author do after he dropped out of college?
   A. He went into business.
   B. He found a job.
   C. He took a calligraphy class.
   D. He went to look for his biological mother.

5. Judging from the author's story, we can infer that _____.
   A. where there's a will, there's a way
   B. opportunity knocks but once
   C. he who hesitates is lost
   D. when one door shuts, another opens in life

II Word Usage

Directions: Complete each of the following sentences with the correct form of the italicized word given in the brackets.

1. We found the program _____ and informative. *(education)*
2. I didn't pay much for this _____ dress. *(expensive)*
3. The job gave her an opportunity to gain _____ experience. *(value)*
4. Mrs. Smith has announced her _____ to retire as manager. *(decide)*
5. The amount that patients are _____ to pay has been raised. *(require)*
6. The conflict needs to be put in its _____ context to be understood. *(history)*
7. I found the talk on healthy eating very _____. *(instruction)*
8. Apparently several buyers have expressed an _____ in the deal. *(interesting)*
9. The money for the flight came out of my _____. *(save)*
10. It was this event that gave _____ to the peace movement. *(born)*

III. Blank Filling

Directions: Translate the Chinese part of the following sentences with the correct form of the words and expressions in the box.

adopt	tuition	romantic	instruction	approach	drop out
turn out	let (sb.) down	make all the difference		graduate	

1. She was injured in the first round and had to _____. (退出比赛)
2. As a writer she takes a completely new _____ to the classic horror story. (采取了一种全新的手法讲述)
3. Having someone to talk to _____ to my mother. (很大变化)
4. He was 18 when he found out he had been _____. (是被领养的)
5. I was a bit late but I couldn't _____ them _____ completely. (不能让他们彻底失望)
6. Candidates should be _____ in science or engineering. (毕业生)
7. It _____ that I was right all along. (结果表明)
8. _____ increased by 5% at universities this year. (学费)
9. Students were given little _____ on the techniques of taking notes. (指导)
10. What could be more _____ than a wedding on a tropical island? (更浪漫的事)

IV. Translation

Directions: Put the following English sentences into Chinese.

1. It was pretty terrible at the time, but looking back it was one of the best decisions I ever made.
2. It was beautiful and historical in a way that science can't show, and I found it interesting.
3. Of course it was impossible to connect the dots looking forward when I was in college. But it was very, very clear looking backwards ten years later.

• Unit 8   Failure and Success •

4. You have to trust in something — your courage, destiny, life, whatever.
5. This approach has never let me down, and it has made all the difference in my life.

V. True or False
Directions: Decide whether the following statements are true or false according to the text. Write "T" if the statement is true and "F" if it is false.

_____1. The writer dropped out of college when he was only a freshman.
_____2. Jobs dropped out because he faced an opportunity of a lifetime.
_____3. Jobs' biological mother didn't finish college, either.
_____4. When he was about 27 years old, Jobs began to design the first computer.
_____5. Jobs' success is due to his trust in himself.

Text B

Before Reading:
1. *How do you understand the saying "Failure is the mother of success."?*
2. *What do you think is the most important factor contributing to a person's success?*

Love and Loss

I was lucky — I found what I loved to do early in life. Woz and I started Apple in my parents' garage when I was 20. In 10 years Apple had grown from just the two of us in a garage into a $2 billion company with over 4000 employees. We had just our finest creation — the Macintosh — when I had just turned 30. And then I got fired. How can you get fired from a company you started? Well, as Apple grew we hired someone whom I thought was very capable to run the company with me, and for the first year or so things went well. But then our ideas of the future began to differ and finally we had a quarrel. When we did, our Board of Directors supported him. So at 30 I was out and it was terrible.

I really didn't know what to do for a few months. I felt that I had disappointed the previous generation of CEOs. I met with them and tried to say sorry for behaving so badly. I was a very public failure, and I

163

even thought about running away. But something slowly began to dawn on me — I still loved what I did. The turn of events at Apple had not changed that one bit. I had been rejected, but I was still in love. And so I decided to start over.

I didn't see it then, but it turned out that getting fired from Apple was the best thing that could have ever happened to me. The heaviness of being successful was replaced by the lightness of being a beginner again. It freed me to enter one of the most creative periods of my life.

During the next five years, I started a company named NeXT, another company named Pixar which went on to create the worlds first computer animated film, and is now the most successful animation studio in the world. Later, a remarkable thing happened because Apple bought NeXT. I returned to Apple, and the technology we developed at NeXT is very important for Apple's success today.

I'm pretty sure none of this would have happened if I hadn't been fired from Apple. It was awful-tasting medicine, but I guess the patient needed it. Sometimes life hits you in the head with a brick. Don't lose faith. I'm convinced that the only thing that kept me going was that I loved what I did. You've got to find what you love. And that is as true for your work as it is for your lovers. Your work is going to fill a large part of your life, and the only way to be truly satisfied is to do what you believe is great work. And the only way to do great work is to love what you do. If you haven't found it yet, keep looking. Don't settle. As with all matters of the heart, you'll know when you find it. And, like any great relationship, it just gets better and better as the years roll on. So keep looking until you find it. Don't settle.

(522 words)

New Words

(标★为A级词汇)

creation	/kriˈeɪʃn/	n.	创造(物);创作(物);作品
turn	/tɜːn/	v.	达到(一定年龄或时间)
		n.	(情况的)变化;转变
fire	/ˈfaɪə(r)/	v.	解雇;开除
hire	/ˈhaɪə(r)/	v.	雇用
capable	/ˈkeɪpəbl/	adj.	有才能的;能干的
differ	/ˈdɪfə(r)/	vi.	不同;相异
board	/bɔːd/	n.	董事会;委员会;理事会
previous	/ˈpriːviəs/	adj.	以前的;先前的
CEO	/ˌsiː iː ˈəʊ/	n.	(= Chief Executive Officer) 首席执行官
★behave	/bɪˈheɪv/	v.	行为;举止
reject	/rɪˈdʒekt/	vt.	丢掉;抛弃
replace	/rɪˈpleɪs/	vt.	代替;取代

Unit 8 Failure and Success

symbol	/ˈsɪmbl/	n.	象征
animated	/ˈænɪmeɪtɪd/	adj.	动画的
studio	/ˈstjuːdiəʊ/	n.	设计室;工作室
remarkable	/rɪˈmɑːkəbl/	adj.	值得注意的;非凡的;显著的
brick	/brɪk/	n.	砖块;砖
faith	/feɪθ/	n.	信心;信任;信念
convinced	/kənˈvɪnst/	adj.	确信的;坚信的;清楚地认识到

Phrases and Expressions

or so	大约……;……左右
Board of Directors	董事会
dawn on	意识到;理解
start over	重新开始

Proper Names

Apple (= Apple Computer Inc.)	美国苹果计算机公司
Macintosh	麦金塔电脑(俗称Mac机或苹果机)
NeXT	NeXT计算机公司(由创办人史蒂夫·乔布斯于1985年被苹果公司辞退后同年成立)
Pixar	皮克斯公司(是一家专门制作电脑动画的公司,其前身是乔治·卢卡斯的电影公司的电脑动画部。1986年被乔布斯收购成立了皮克斯动画工作室。)

Exercises

I. Summary

Directions: Fill in the blanks with the appropriate words according to your understanding.

When I was 20, Woz and I started Apple. In 10 years, it had grown from a two-person (1) _____ into a $2 billion company with over 4000 employees. When I just (2) _____ 30, we (3) _____ the Macintosh. But later I got (4) _____ from the company I started. At first, I really didn't know what to do. I even thought about running (5) _____. However, I still love what I did even though I had been (6) _____. And so, I decided to start (7) _____. During the next five years, I started another company named NeXT, which was bought by Apple later. I returned to Apple, and the technology we (8) _____ at NeXT is very important for Apple success today. Sometimes life hit you in the head with a brick. Don't lose (9) _____. I'm

(10) _____ that the only thing that kept me going was that I loved what I did. So you've got to find what you love.

II. Reading Comprehension

Directions: Fill in the blanks of the following two statements according to the text.

1. The heaviness of being successful was _____ by the lightness of being a _____ again. It freed me to enter one of the most _____ periods of my life.
2. Your work is going to _____ a large part of your life and the only way to be truly _____ is to do what you believe is great work. And the only way to do great work is to _____ what you do.

III. Vocabulary & Structures

Directions: Fill in the blanks with the proper expressions in the box below.

| creation | hire | capable | differ | previous |
| behave | replace | faith | convinced | or so |

1. Email has largely _____ the traditional business letter.
2. I was impressed by his _____ handling of the situation.
3. They spent an hour _____ searching for the missing file.
4. Disney's _____ brought joy to children everywhere.
5. Despite all my father's arguments, I still wasn't _____.
6. His main responsibility is _____ and firing.
7. The techniques used _____ from company to company.
8. She was embarrassed at having _____ in such a childish way.
9. This issue was discussed in the _____ chapter.
10. I'm delighted to know you have such _____ in me.

IV. Translation

Directions: Put the following English sentences into Chinese.

1. Nothing great was ever achieved without enthusiasm.
2. No road of flowers leads to glory.
3. He that falls today may rise tomorrow.
4. Success belongs to the persevering.
5. Well is it known that ambition can creep as well as soar.

Unit 8 Failure and Success

Part III Strategies

阅读解析(四)

简答题和 Task 3 摘要题同属识别细节题。考生应首先认真阅读短文,然后根据所提问题寻找所需信息。注意答案不能超过 3 个单词。这就要求我们找到关键词,并剔除与关键词无关的其它词,以确保信息的准确性。

【例】2011 年 6 月实考题

Requirements for All Employees

1. Within ten minutes of arrival, be in uniform and at your work station. Breaks should not be longer than the time allowed, and restroom and smoke breaks need to be part of the break periods, not in addition to them.
2. Work dress should be clean and professional (职业的) each working day.
3. All employees are responsible for cleaning any workstation.
4. Work tasks are given daily, and may be changed during service as needed. Employees are expected to be flexible when receiving the tasks given.
5. When tasks are completed, the employees are expected to clean the areas around their workstations. Wiping all tables and counters off, cleaning the floor and under the tables, as well as wiping off the cooler door and also things that should be done when time allows.

Directions: Here are some requirements for employees working for a restaurant. After reading them, you are required to complete the questions. You should write your answers in no more than 3 words.

1) What should the employees do within 10 minutes after they arrive?
   Be in _____ and at their workplaces.
   答案在员工守则第一条中的第一句, Within ten minutes of arrival, be in uniform and at your work station. 因此答案是 uniform。

2) What are the rules about the restroom and smoke breaks?
   They are regarded as part of _____.
   答案也在第一条中的第二句, Breaks should not be longer than the time allowed, and restroom and smoke breaks need to be part of the break periods, not in addition to them. 因此答案是 the break periods。

3) What is the requirement about the employees' work dress?
   Their work dress should be _____.
   答案在守则中的第二条, Work dress should be clean and professional (职业的) each working day, 因此答案是 clean and professional。

4) What are employees expected to do when they receive work tasks?
   They are expected to be _____.
   答案在守则的第四条中的第二句 Employees are expected to be flexible when receiving

the tasks given, 因此答案是 flexible。

5) What should the employees do when they complete their tasks?
They are required to _____ around their workstations.
答案在守则中的第五条, When tasks are completed, the employees are expected to clean the areas around their workstations, 因此答案是 clean the areas。

Practice 1:

Directions: The following is about how to write an abstract. After reading it, you should give a brief answer to the 5 questions (No. 1 through No. 5) that follow. The answers should be written in no more than 3 words.

The rules for writing an abstract (摘要) are almost the same to those for writing the summary of an investigation report. In an abstract you (1) make an outline of the problem and the purpose of your investigation, (2) mention very briefly how you conducted the investigation or tests, (3) describe your main findings, and (4) make the conclusions. These must be done in as few words as possible; ideally, your abstract will be about 125 words long and never more than 250 words.

From the abstract, readers must be able to decide whether the information you provide in the scientific paper or report is particularly interesting to them and whether they should read further. Because a scientific paper is written for readers who generally are familiar with your technical or scientific discipline (学科), you may use technical terminology (术语) in the abstract. The abstract should be written last, when the whole paper has been written, so that you can make an abstract of the brief details you need from what you have already written.

1. How should you write an abstract?
   You should write it in as _____ as possible.
2. What should be described in the abstract?
   Our _____.
3. What are the readers likely to do if they find the abstract interesting?
4. Why can you use technical terminology in the abstract?
   Because our readers are usually _____ our scientific discipline.
5. When should you write the abstract?
   After you have finished _____.

Practice 2:

Directions: There is an advertisement below. After reading it, you should give a brief answer to the 5 questions (No. 1 through No. 5) that follow. The answers should be written in no more than 3 words.

Toshiba Simplifies Success

Getting ahead in business has never been easy. But office equipment you can count on can make success easier to reach. And you can always count on Toshiba office equipment.

You can rely on our phone system that can expand along with your business. You can rely on our printers that deliver clear documents day in and day out. And our copiers that come in the size and with the features just right for any office.

Unit 8　Failure and Success

And we have even more to offer. All our office equipment is designed to be as flexible and timesaving as possible. Like our laptop computers, they have the power of desktops but are portable. So you can take our office equipment anywhere. Their advanced memory has the ability to remember and even correct documents to make faxing easier.

Simple concepts that are Toshiba's guiding philosophies.

In Touch With Us Tomorrow
TOSHIBA

1. What is the main idea of this passage?
   It is _____ supplied by Toshiba that make you more successful.
2. What is the main equipment Toshiba supplies? _____.
3. What is Toshiba's office designed to be?
   It is designed to be as _____ as possible.
4. Compared with other faxing machines, Toshiba's has the ability to remember and _____.
5. What does "In Touch With Us Tomorrow" mean?
   It means _____ and have contact with us.

Part IV　Applied Writing

Memo（备忘录）

备忘录是一种简易公文，它是公司各部门之间广泛应用的一种书面联系手段，主要用来传递信息，提醒对方或表明自己的看法。

备忘录一般由以下六个部分组成：

1. 抬头（Memo）
2. 发函人姓名（From: xxx）
3. 收函人姓名（To: xxx）
4. 日期（Date）
5. 标题（Subject / Re）
6. 正文（Body or Message）

Sample:

Memo

To: Miss Jackson
From: Daniel Smith, General Manager
Date: Jan. 18, 2002
Re: Complaints

Message:
   I received this complaint letter from one of our regular customers this morning. Please pass it on to our Sales Manager as soon as possible. Urge him to take care of it and give me a satisfactory solution.

Assignment: Write a memo of no less than 100 words according to the given information.

公司每年举办的圣诞晚会今年将会推迟到一月中旬。请以人力资源部经理Mary Brown的名义写一份备忘录通知全体员工，内容包括：
- 通知晚会推迟事宜
- 说明原因
- 代表公司表达歉意

Part V Cultural Express

Apple

Apple Inc. (formerly **Apple Computer, Inc.**) is an American multinational corporation that designs and sells consumer electronics, computer software, and personal computers. The company's best-known hardware products are the Macintosh line of computers, the iPod, the iPhone and the iPad. Its software includes the Mac OS X operating system; the iTunes media browser; the iLife suite of multimedia and creativity software; the iWork suite of productivity software; Aperture, a professional photography package; Final Cut Studio, a suite of professional audio and film-industry software products; Logic Studio, a suite of music production tools; the Safari web browser; and iOS, a mobile operating system.

As of July 2011, Apple has 364 retail stores in thirteen countries, and an online store. It competes with Exxon Mobile as the largest publicly traded company in the world by market capitalization, as well as the largest technology company in the

Unit 8 Failure and Success

world by revenue and profit, more than Google and Microsoft combined. As of September 24, 2011, the company had 60,400 permanent full-time employees and 2,900 temporary full-time employees worldwide; its worldwide annual revenue in 2010 totaled $65 billion, growing to $108 billion in 2011.

Fortune magazine named Apple the most admired company in the United States in 2008, and in the world from 2008 to 2012. However, the company has received widespread criticism for its contractors' labor, and for its environmental and business practices.

Established on April 1, 1976 in Cupertino, California, and incorporated January 3, 1977, the company was named Apple Computer, Inc. for its first 30 years. The word "Computer" was removed from its name on January 9, 2007.

拓展词汇

成语

1. Losers are always in the wrong. / Nothing succeeds like success.
   成则为王,败则为寇。
2. fall short of success for lack of a final effort 功亏一篑
3. give up halfway / leave something unfinished 半途而废
4. fail on the verge of success / suffer defeat when victory is within reach 功败垂成
5. Nothing ventured, nothing gained. 不入虎穴,焉得虎子。
6. invincible position 不败之地
7. gain an immediate victory / win instant success 马到成功
8. Constant dropping can wear the stone. 滴水穿石。
9. eager for instant success and quick profits 急功近利
10. When conditions are ripe, success is achieved. 水到渠成。
11. trust to chance and strokes of luck 守株待兔
12. reach the goal in one step / accomplish one's aim in one move 一蹴而就

13. A thousand-li journey is started by taking the first step. 千里之行,始于足下。
14. not easy to come by / hard-earned 来之不易
15. attain a high of perfection 炉火纯青

名人名言

Failure is the mother of success. — Thomas Paine
失败乃成功之母。 托马斯·潘恩
The unexamined life is not worth living. — Socrates
混混噩噩的生活不值得过。 苏格拉底
Our destiny offers not the cup of despair, but the chalice of opportunity. So let us seize it, not in fear, but in gladness. — R.M. Nixon
命运给予我们的不是失望之酒,而是机会之杯。因此,让我们毫无畏惧,满心愉悦地把握命运。 尼克松
Living without an aim is like sailing without a compass. — John Ruskin
生活没有目标,犹如航海没有罗盘。 罗斯金
What makes life dreary is the want of motive. — George Eliot
没有了目的,生活便郁闷无光。 乔治·埃略特
Towering genius disdains a beaten path. It seeks regions hitherto unexplored. — Lincoln
卓越的天才不屑走旁人走过的路。他寻找迄今未开拓的地区。 林肯
There is no such thing as a great talent without great will-power. — Balzac
没有伟大的意志力,便没有雄才大略。 巴尔扎克
Fear not that the life shall come to an end, but rather fear that it shall never have a beginning. — J. H. Newman
不要害怕你的生活将要结束,应该担心你的生活永远不会真正开始。 纽曼
Gods determine what you're going to be. — Julius Erving
人生的奋斗目标决定你将成为怎样的人。 欧文
An aim in life is the only fortune worth finding. — Robert Louis Stevenson
生活的目标,是唯一值得寻找的财富。 罗伯特·路易斯·史蒂文森
Try not to become a man of success but rather try to become a man of value. — A. Einstein
不要为成功而努力,要为做一个有价值的人而努力。 爱因斯坦
You have to believe in yourself. That's the secret of success. — Charles Chaplin
人必须有自信,这是成功的秘密。 卓别林